WHAT IS IT LIKE
TO DIE?

"I floated away from my body, away from my cares and troubles . . . What I came to was comforting; it was the best thing that ever happened to me . . . I pulled out of my body. It was like a blue-gray mist which floated up right next to the ceiling. I could see them work on my own body. I felt like a transformation. I didn't like being dragged back to my body, but once I entered my body, everything seemed all right. This new knowledge has gotten me excited about life again. . ."

From *Journey To The Other Side*

JOURNEY TO THE OTHER SIDE

by DAVID R. WHEELER

ace books

A Division of Charter Communications Inc.
A GROSSET & DUNLAP COMPANY
1120 Avenue of the Americas
New York, New York 10036

JOURNEY TO THE OTHER SIDE—ACE EDITION

Copyright © 1976, 1977 by David R. Wheeler

Published simultaneously in Canada

An ACE Book

Printed in U.S.A.

CONTENTS

1
A PERSONAL GLIMPSE
AT THE OTHER SIDE

I died for an instant. My encounter with death was brief and overwhelmingly pleasant. My experience with the other side of this life made such a great impact on me that after twenty years I remember it vividly.

Twenty years ago my parents took me to visit my grandparents, deep in the heavily wooded area of northern Louisiana. There I developed pneumonia and had to be taken to a hospital in Shreveport. By the time I was admitted to the hospital, I had a high fever and was breathing with great difficulty. After several days in the hospital, I was weak and close to death.

At some point during that time I realized that I was going to die. My perception of the world around me changed. The bright, sunlit hospital room turned dark and seemed lit only by dying embers of an unseen fire. Objects in the room were mere wisps of their former substance. My bed, the covers, and the nightstand a few inches from my head seemed painted a dull, orange-red color.

I heard soft rustling, but I could not tell if the sounds were figments of my imagination or the whispers of spirits nearby.

My awareness of the room dimmed, and the world immediately around me became like a tunnel with walls that glowed with a slight orange-red, reflected light. The tunnel felt warm and cozy. It was like watching the glow of the fire in a ski lodge after being out in the cold all day. The fire draws you into it and makes you feel secure.

As I lay in the hospital bed, the room became still darker, the tunnel grew longer. Noises and conversations around me faded away; I did not hear my labored breathing anymore. Suddenly I felt very good. Then, I felt a change occur within me. Such a change had never happened before that moment and has not happened since. But I remember it clearly.

I felt myself moving away from my physical body. I perceived a distinct separation from my body. It was not like dreaming, nor was it a hallucination. I just knew intuitively that one part of me was moving away from the other part. I was not frightened. It was a good feeling. I started to float just a little distance above my body.

Shadows at the end of the tunnel were speaking, but I could barely discern the faint whispers. The voices were saying, ''How is he?'' I did not care that they were talking about me. I just wanted to drift away.

I had no grasp of the passage of time. The pressure I had felt in attempting to breathe was replaced by a complete lack of awareness of my breathing. I no longer needed to breathe.

I continued to see several hazy figures slowly moving

about at the end of the tunnel and I could hear parts of their conversation.

"How is he?"

"He's in bad shape."

I lost interest in the conversation and the physical world. I felt a comforting change in consciousness. I did not drift into a dream state nor did I pass out. Things around me faded away; I did not hear my labored breathing anymore. Suddenly I felt very good. Then, I felt a me, I became a part of the world. Without any physical perceptions, I simply knew and understood what was taking place. Unafraid, I knew that I was dying.

The complete departure of my spirit from the physical body came as no surprise to me. It was pleasant—so strange yet perfectly acceptable. It was as if I knew all along that this process was possible and when it actually occurred, life and the hereafter held no secrets. I became at the same time both an integral part and an observer. I was a form without corporeal substance. Without looking down from where I was, I knew that my own body lay upon the hospital bed.

It was a transcendental glimpse of another existence. Then back again.

The flickering flame which had seemed to be drawing me to it suddenly vanished. I recognized the people who were standing around my bed discussing my condition. One voice belonged to my physician and the other was my Mother's tearful voice. I wanted to live again. I returned to my body and asked them, "May I have a glass of water?" My ephemeral journey to the Other Side had ended.

Many people have had deeply emotional responses to

similar experiences of dying. Some have become devoutly religious. I have become a very interested observer and student of "thanatology," which includes study of the reports of persons who have been clinically dead and then resuscitated.

Throughout our lives, things happen to us within certain contexts which are instrumental in coloring our view of events around us and shaping our behavioral responses to life. Those lasting responses may be focused around a simple happening—a quick smile from a stranger—or something more complex—the death of a loved one.

Outstanding events in our lives do not always remain part of our conscious being, but they reside just below in the layers of the subconscious. Like gently guiding hands, subconscious thoughts may channel our perceptions and ideas.

It was not until I began to read and hear stories of others who had had experiences similar to mine that I decided that there was really something significant in my experience of floating out of my body.

My view of the Other Side was also influenced by an article in *Reader's Digest*, which described the experiences of a man who had been dead for twenty-three minutes and was resuscitated. What fascinated me about the story was the similarity to what I had been through. Victor Solow's article, "I Died at 10:52 A.M.," is a very moving and graphic account of one man's view of the Other Side, and I was gratified to be able to interview him for this book.

On April 25, 1976, the *New York Times* carried an article entitled "Approach to Life After Death," by Tom Ferrell and Donald Johnston. It said that the investigations of leading scientists have suggested ". . . some intriguing possibilities concerning such matters as the clinical definition of death and whether the nature of the death experience is of this world or otherworldly."

The *New York Times* article removed the shroud of embarrassment that seemed to surround my curiosity about my own experience. Talking to others who had had similar feelings of floating out of the body, of being in a tunnel, and contentment and happiness at being dead led me to think that there was more to my view of the Other Side than just a hallucination or a temporary mental aberration. After interviewing many people who have been through clinical death and had experiences like mine, I now believe that my spirit actually transcended my physical body for a brief time. I know that I died and caught a glimpse of the Other Side.

Dr. Raymond A. Moody, a practicing psychiatrist, has spent five years interviewing patients who have experienced clinical death and been resuscitated and he has written about the subject in *Life After Life*. Dr. Moody has come to believe in the survival of the spirit after the death of the human body. He appeared on Barry Farber's late-night talk show on radio station WOR in New York City on May 20, 1976 and described some aspects of the hereafter as related to him by his patients. Moody noted one big problem that many had in describing their experiences: "Words are only vague analogies for what they felt while they were dead. They had their greatest difficulty describing their spirits' shape and form." Almost all of the patients were resentful that they had been brought back to life. Death was a much better condition.

One of Dr. Moody's patients described his unhappiness

about coming back to life as follows: "After I came back, I cried off and on for about a week because I had to live in this world. After seeing that one, I didn't want to come back."

It is difficult to write about death. Usually we do not learn much about the experience from the person who has died. Therefore, most discussions hinge instead on the personal experience of mourning. This is the case in D. H. Lawrence's *Sons and Lovers*. In one scene, a character is upset at the death of his mother and the reader is asked to identify with his feelings as he mourns.

> She lay like a maiden asleep . . . He bent over her . . . She was young again . . . She would wake up. She would lift her eyelids. She was with him still.
>
> He bent and kissed her passionately. But there was a coldness about the mouth. He bit his lip in horror. Looking at her, he felt that he could never, never let her go. No! He stroked the hair from her temples. That, too, was cold. He saw the mouth so dumb and wondering at the hurt. Then he crouched on the floor whispering to her: 'Mother, mother!"
>
> He was still with her when the undertakers came, young men who had been to school with him.

In this evocation of death only the son's grief is expressed.

Some people are terriby frightened at the prospect of facing death. Others find even worse the prospect of having to die without knowledge as to what lies on the Other Side—or if there is anything at all.

One way of learning about the next world is to make the

trip yourself and observe firsthand. Some do exactly that—they kill themselves. The rate of suicides in the United States in 1973 was 12 deaths per 100,000 people. That year the deaths of 24,440 people were listed as suicides. The figure probably does not accurately indicate the number of people who, in the final analysis, killed themselves. Some portion of the more than one million people dying of heart disease ate and smoked themselves to death. Many traffic accidents reflect the suicidal tendencies of the victims who drove too fast or drank themselves to their deaths. So there is, indeed, a great eagerness among some unhappy people to see what lurks on the Other Side.

This book is a small peek under the heavy, black curtain surrounding death which is usually entered only through a one-way door, not through a revolving door as in my case. I have actually experienced death and I have talked with others who have had similar experiences. I have studied the accounts of people who have ideas of what to expect on the Other Side. I have talked with religious leaders and research scientists who have something important to say about the next world. We all find the same thing—there seems to be something on the Other Side!

2
ONE MAN'S JOURNEY
TO THE OTHER SIDE

Some individuals have given fascinating accounts of the continuation of their existence on the other side of this life. There seems to be something like a spiritual transformation and reawakening of the human soul.

Victor Solow had his heart attack while he and his wife were stopped for a traffic signal. His heart stopped and he quit breathing. As he turned blue, his wife ran for help. Time was essential if he was to survive.

In humans, lack of oxygen in the blood for ten seconds causes unconsciousness, and in only thirty seconds the electrical activity of the cortex ceases. Then, if the much-needed oxygen is not delivered to the brain's cells within three to five minutes, irreversible brain damage occurs.

Of course, there are innumerable instances of "clinically" dead patients being revived after cessation of their cardiac and respiratory activities. This is usually possible when the victim is lucky enough to be near an emergency room or intensive care unit of a hospital so that life-saving techniques and equipment can be quickly employed.

Victor Solow experienced "clinical" death for twenty-three minutes. He had no respiration, no heartbeat. He had quit living. Solow was miles from the nearest hospital, but only seconds away from him was a police officer, a trained medical squad, and life-keeping oxygen apparatus. Within three minutes of the stoppage of his heart, Solow was given cardiopulmonary resuscitation. Although he remained technically dead for twenty-three minutes, Solow's brain was supplied with oxygen by the mechanical and external pressures of heart massage.

Victor Solow was dead upon arrival at the hospital. There was no pulse, no breathing, no vital signs of any kind. Electric shock was administered several times before he was revived.

But for days after the accident Solow could not seem to get his spirit to stay within his body. It kept popping out. The physicians called this "retrograde amnesia."

Finally Solow got together with himself.

When I telephoned and asked if I could interview him for my book on people's experiences while clinically dead, I was somewhat amazed when he agreed to see me the following morning.

I interviewed a very normal and very happy individual. Solow looks a young forty, not at all like someone who was dead for an eternity.

"I experienced timelessness while I was dead. It was a very private moment, but I wanted to write about it so that others could become somewhat more aware of my experiences."

I asked about the response to his *Reader's Digest* article.

"They were all beautiful letters. I got several thousand of them from people all over the world. They were positive. Some of the writers attempted to explain the meaning of what had happened."

I asked about those interpretations.

Solow replied. "One of the letters said, 'Jesus Christ gave you this experience for a purpose. You have been chosen and you are an important person. You must carry the message to all.' "

I wondered if he had felt a need to become an evangelical preacher, to tell of his experiences with the Other Side.

"Not at all. I have no intention of attempting to convince others of my experiences. In fact, I really to not care if they believe me. I *know* what happened, and there is no way that I can make others share my experiences or make them believe my story."

We talked for a long time. About midway through our conversation, Solow received a telephone call from his daughter. The tone of the conversation showed the great love between the two.

I asked, "Have you always been so happy and at ease?"

"Before my heart arrest, I was always pretty tense and unhappy with the world. After experiencing death, my relationship with this life has become more meaningful."

I asked about Solow's perception of the Other Side, whether or not he perceived good and evil as being inherent in the hereafter.

"I don't believe that there is any difference to be found in people. I can't see there being a heaven as opposed to a hell. I just see one existence which supplants this one once we die.

"I really do not think that we perceive the universe around us as it actually exists."

Solow went on to explain his attitude toward another state of consciousness. "Our upbringings have taught us to misperceive the world.

"I believe that it was at the very instant when I felt myself die that I started moving at very high speed toward a net of great luminosity and brilliance. The universe had no other forms, shapes, or things in it than me and the giant net, which was like a huge tennis net strung across the vastness of the universe from eternity to eternity. There were knots on the net where the thing came together. These modal points connecting the elements of the net were vibrating with an intense form of energy—pure, raw energy."

I could tell that Solow was having extreme difficulty in describing what he had experienced while clinically dead. The words came slowly, and he kept repeating that it was impossible to adequately explain what he had felt. But at no time did he let his inability to describe his experience shake his faith in what had happened to him.

"I truly entered another reality the instant I died. It was so different from this life's experiences that it cannot be translated or explained to another person. Try telling someone who is blind what a Renoir looks like. My experience can't be understood except through the actual experience of death itself.

"The way in which I related to the giant, vibrating net was new. It was understanding something in a totally unique way. In a way that we don't have with this frame of reference or our present methods of perceptions.

"My perception of the universe that I was flying through was beyond our sensory experiences here in this

11

reality. The void of the universe was around me and formed a backdrop for the pulsating grid. The universal void was without color, but I cannot describe it as even being black. It was something else entirely. Maybe it was a total absence of light, either emitted or reflected.

"The universe's color and substance was something other than what I'd seen in my lifetime of experiences. It was something else.

"I work in the area of films, and I know a lot about composition and that sort of thing, but what I experienced was unlike anything of earth. I cannot explain it. I cannot describe it. And I cannot deal with it. There is no truth nor is there any validity to it—but I *know* the experience."

I wanted a little more description of the Other Side. He answered:

"Can you describe music? I can tell you the difference between the Rolling Stones and Bach. That will not do. Find a dead person and try to show him or explain what Bach sounds like. When you can do that, then I might be able to relate to you the experiences which I had in another reality."

Did he ever reach the net, I asked.

"I felt as I approached that huge grid that it wasn't something that I should be doing, but I had no control over the events as they were happening to me. I just was swept along, and I don't think I had any way of stopping the inevitable."

Time passed while Solow sought the words that would best convey his approach to the grid.

"For a brief time I felt myself appear to slow down in my approach to that tremendous cold energy of the grid. The net's strands and knots were still brightly luminous and continuing to vibrate with a cold energy. Then I became part of the grid.

"A second transformation occurred once I made contact with that grid. My first transformation was when my spirit, or essence, left my body and was hurled through space toward the barrier. Then this second transformation took place. Whatever I was before contacting the grid was suddenly drained, absorbed, and changed—all at the same instant. But it was not painful; nor was it frightening. It was not a burning sensation. It was not like freezing. It merely consumed me."

At this point we talked for a while about other things because Solow's hesitancy indicated that he was having trouble finding words to explain what happened in the grid. Then he continued.

"The grid could have been similar to an electrical transformer which changes electricity in one circuit and puts it into another circuit. The giant grid converted me and transformed me beyond all concepts of space and time.

"It was this absence of being in a place or the lack of the passage of time which is the hardest to describe. I was completely changed. I became an altered 'I,' the barest essence of my former self. From out of my lifetime of fears, hopes, and worries emerged, or was transformed, a new 'I.' I became an indestructible—pure spirit and pure energy.

"But I was not a separate entity anymore, for I had become part of the universe. I fitted in perfectly and harmoniously. My spirit became quiet and still. I needed nothing any longer."

Solow's journey to the Other Side was incomplete.

"I did feel like there was something else out there. I don't know what it was, nor how to describe it. But I really felt at the time that there was something outstanding just about to happen when I felt a huge slap, and I suddenly returned to the table on which my body was lying in the emergency room. I know a further revelation was about to occur when they resuscitated me and brought me back to this world."

An unknown force awaits him on his next trip to the Other Side.

After mentioning the abrupt change, Solow's thoughts seemed to linger on his twenty-three-minute experience in the hereafter.

"I was as different as my own fingerprints, while at the same time I was completely part of this new world and universe. There was little time for thought, no time for fear. And then I left this wonderful place.

"I was in a state of transitional condition. I still suffer from a recurring longing for that state, but many of my attitudes about the world have changed and continue to change.

"I don't think that my return to this existence was completed all at once. For the first few days after my resuscitation, I was very amused at the way my body functioned. I was absentminded. My family and the doctors felt that I had suffered brain damage. I was detached from myself. How strange it seemed to reach out for something like a glass of water. Eating seemed totally new to me.

"Every once in a while the vibrating grid becomes a vivid picture in my mind, and I think about how I became part of another existence. I know what death will be like. It has taught me to appreciate my experiences in this life.

"It is important to transcend our preconceived views of this universe. Each person has within him the necessary powers that will enable him to alter his self so that the spirit can emerge. This is a part of each person.

"I brought something out of the brush with death—the idea that life should be experienced. We go through this realm for some purpose. Maybe it is to do good deeds, to have many children, or to experience all that the world has to offer."

Others have spoken of their greater zest for living after having been close to death or actually dead for a moment. Another reporter has said, "One sometimes has to die in order to experience life. After they resuscitated me, I decided to savor the experiences of life."

Psychologically, we know that human beings need a wide variety of experiences in their lives for their own mental health.

William James, the famous American psychologist and philosopher, once pointed out that there are two types of experiences in life. There is "knowledge of" and there is "knowledge about." The first is knowledge gained through experiences, such as being clinically dead and then revived. The second is knowledge resulting from an interested study and reflection on a topic. Experience may well be the best teacher, but in this world we must learn about the Other Side in the second way.

A physician who had treated terminally ill cancer patients for ten years summed up the remarks of dying patients. "They all say about the same thing. It boils down to this: 'Doctor, I know my time is ending. I regret really only two things. One is not doing enough in my life. I never traveled enough. I did not take time to see the world around me. The second is that I regret those things which I did *not* do.' "

Victor Solow's experience with the Other Side has given him a tremendous thirst for life, so that he will not have a great many regrets about things he did not do.

3
THE PROFOUND CHANGES

"The death experience is beautiful. I liked it when it occurred. I even struggled against being brought back to this life. The experience is something I'd like to feel again. It completely changed the way I see myself and those around me. It changed my life for the better."

This view closely parallels hundreds of reports from individuals who have been dead or very close to dying.

The experience of dying—including "clinical" death, near-death due to accidents, freezing, drowning, car wrecks, and out-of-body travels—usually alter rather drastically a person's philosophical approach to life, his religious views, and, of course, belief in life after death.

Fred K., a businessman, had become listless and completely bored with life. Nothing interested him. Politics, business, sex—all had lost flavor for him. The joy of living had gone out of him.

Then one day Fred K. had a heart attack. He was clinically dead upon arrival at the emergency room.

Physicians were able to bring him back to life with adrenaline and electric shock to the heart.

Fred describes his experience in glowing terms.

"I floated away from my body, away from my cares and troubles, and off this world. What I came to was comforting; it was the best thing that has ever happened to me. I really enjoyed the feeling of dying.

"I pulled out of my body. It was like a blue-gray mist which floated up right next to the ceiling. I could see them work on my own body. I felt a transformation.

"I didn't like being dragged back to my body, but once I entered my body, everything seemed all right.

"I used to find nothing worthwhile in living. When I died and came back, I really got to believe in the hereafter. This knowledge has sure got me excited about life again.

"Dying is great. Living is exciting."

Fred's family physician conducted an examination of him a few weeks after Fred was released from the hospital. "The patient showed a complete change in his psychological outlook. He had really become a pleasure to be with."

Helen A. had been Fred's business associate. She later said, "Fred and I used to have dinner together to discuss business matters. I never had any trouble with him before, unless it was keeping him awake and interested in the work.

"It was about a week after he got out of the hospital that we went out for supper one night. I thought it was to discuss business. But I was totally wrong. He wanted a lot more.

"There was a change in the man. What died was an old man who had forgotten the zest in living. What had been reborn was a sex fiend. He got excited about, and chased after all the ladies. I went out with him after his stay in the hospital thinking that he wanted to discuss the business with me. Instead, he was all over me. Death sure transformed his personality. He had a new outlook on life—and on me."

Later, a much happier seventy-seven-year-old man got out of the business world. He now lives in the sunshine of Florida. You could say that Fred had been through a spiritual rebirth and been born again.

Sam was a senile, ninety-six-year-old man who died and was resuscitated. When he came back to life there was a remarkable improvement in his ability to function and his senility had faded. It was as if a vacuum cleaner had removed all the cobwebs from his mind.

Sam's nurse told me, "The old guy was a real pain. He could do only those things which would cause us the greatest amount of trouble. Like ask for water all the time. But he couldn't feed himself. He was a lot of trouble for all of us."

He died during an operation. The doctor quickly moved into action by giving injections and hitting the heart with adrenaline. They worked on him for a long time. After they thought they had lost him, Sam flickered back to life and asked, "What are you all doing to me? Can't a man die in peace?"

Later, nurses jokingly inquired whether the doctors should have brought him back since he had been so difficult before the operation.

The surprise came when the patient was taken from the intensive care unit and was placed in another wing of the hospital. His thinking ability was markedly changed. He was a new old man. Delightful, full of spirit, cleaned out of the cobwebs. Although he had only a fleeting remembrance of the experience, Sam was a changed person.

In 1971, Janet Y. was rushed to the hospital in critical condition after taking a lethal number of pills. For a brief period of time, she was clinically "dead." Temporary death transformed Janet's life also.

"I really got tired of living, and I killed myself. What I saw while I was dead was so beautiful. Something happened. After they brought me back, I wanted to live again. I think I saw heaven close-up for a while. It was real, not a dream or a movie."

I have been able to piece together the story of this seventeen-year-old girl who killed herself. I discussed the facts of her case with the attending physicians, her psychologist, therapists, nurses, and the emergency room employees and nurses.

The girl's psychologist is concerned lest the patient lapse back into her depressive, pre-suicide state. "My death experience is still a vivid recollection." She remembers her experience clearly. "It is not something which fades away and is forgotten. It'll always be there to affect the way I see things."

The girl was discovered near death in a basement apartment. She was in very bad condition from an overdose of drugs and slashed wrists.

The dead girl was brought into the emergency room. A code-call went out to summon the necessary life-giving teams. They worked over her for a long period of time.

Janet reports:

"I had this beautiful feeling. I was floating up in the air and watching things happen below. There was a group of people dressed in light green clothes standing around a body which was laying on a table. I suddenly recognized that body. It was me: The people were trying to bring me back to life. I didn't want them to do it. I was so happy being dead.

"I had a feeling of traveling at great speed down this long tunnel. I could see a bright light at the end. I entered the light. It was like a fast train. Then, I was there in the bright light. I was part of it. There were others there in the light. I didn't see them. I just knew that they were around me, and it made me feel good. I was not afraid anymore.

"I felt completely at ease. I wasn't worried with my problems any longer. I have never been religious. I don't know about God and those kinds of things. After the doctors got me back to life, I feel differently about heaven. I think I got pretty close to it."

Most unsuccessful suicides report a continuation of their problems while they are clinically dead. They describe negative and unhappy feelings. This was not the case with Janet. Her death experience altered her view toward her problems in a positive manner.

"I had a great experience during my death. I could actually feel a splitting of myself out of my body."

The young girl who had killed herself did have something similar to a religious transformation or spiritual awakening as the result of her death experience. Somehow the process of dying, experiencing the Other Side, and then being brought back, has altered her perspective on this life. Janet decided to try another approach to living and the change is remarkable. Her psychologist is amazed at her progress.

There seems to be something—a spirit, the soul, or an altered state of consciousness—which continues to exist after the death of the human body. People who have experienced clinical death and have been resuscitated, report an almost impossible-to-describe warmth and happiness while they were dead. Many report leaving their bodies like a wisp of cloud and floating near the ceiling. As they float, they recognize their bodies and they also are aware of the presence of other "beings" in the form of spirits or bright lights. They have even watched the doctors in their efforts to bring life back to the body.

The experiences of visitors to the Other Side have brought about various kinds of changes. Depressions have been erased; suicidal tendencies have been replaced with happier feelings; and the cobwebs of senility have been swept away and replaced by clearer thinking.

4
VISIONS IN DYING

"The best parts of my life flashed before me as I was hurled through the air toward my death. I saw all my old girl friends. I remember scenes of things we used to do together. It didn't take long. The car backed in front of me, I slammed into the side of it with my motorcycle, and I flew over the car and landed on the concrete and asphalt twenty to thirty feet away. It was in that time I was in the air that I watched the best parts of my life."

Joe Don's story of his "flash of life" before what he thought was his certain death is a common one with the hundreds of other people who have come very close to accidental death. It is like a replay of the major events in the person's life.

Joe Don felt certain that he was going to die. Somehow his mind responded to this fact in a detached fashion. He relived highlights of his past while waiting to die.

"I remembered my girl friends—almost all of them flashed in front of my eyes. I saw them and some of the things we used to do. I don't remember hearing them talk; I remember only seeing their faces and bodies."

Joe Don described at length one of the scenes from his "flash of life" as follows:

"I remember vividly this one scene. It was about Carol, a girl I really liked. We had been caught in this sudden downpour in my Austin Healy convertible. I had the top stored in the trunk and by the time I could get it out, we were completely soaked.

"I watched myself get frustrated in trying to get the top on the car. It came completely off and you folded it up. It was impossible to get it on in a hurry. I gave up after working on it for several moments and joined Carol under a tree. It didn't keep the rain off, but we had a great time holding each other.

"There were other girls and other visions that flashed through my mind on my way to my death."

Dr. Russell Noyes, Professor of Psychiatry at the University of Iowa's College of Medicine, has, for years, been interviewing patients like Joe Don who have come very close to death. The impressions of these individuals who think that they are surely going to die within seconds have revealed something which Dr. Noyes calls the "depersonalization syndrome." This phenomenon commonly occurs in life-threatening situations. The reaction can be broken down into three stages: resistance, review, and transcendence.

During the first stage the victim's awareness of the situation is greatly enhanced. The person becomes more alert to the dangerous environment. Mental and physical powers increase. There have been reports of people being able to lift cars and bend steel with their bare hands when death seemed imminent.

If the danger and fear of death is not overcome, the individual resigns himself to his fate. Profound tranquility sets in and, according to Dr. Noyes, the person enters the second stage.

Fred R. was involved in a car wreck. Just before impact, he appraised the situation.

"I knew that I was as good as dead. There was not anything that I could do anymore, so I quit struggling and let it happen. It was like going to a movie and watching someone get killed on the screen. I did not care one way or another."

In this second stage of detachment, the victim suddenly becomes an innocent bystander who watches his own forthcoming death with complacency. During this stage, the victim also sees his past flash before his eyes.

Dr. Noyes said, "This component of the depersonalization syndrome is called panoramic memory. It is only one feature of the entire process."

He continued, "I find the case about Joe Don who relived his previous experiences with the girls most interesting. He obviously was enjoying his death experience.

"I do wonder about this phenomenon really being a reaction to the threat of death. There are many other causes which bring forth the same responses, such as depressions, schizophrenia, temporal lobe epilepsy and, of course, the use of certain drugs. The phenomenon is not specific to dying."

Twenty-five percent of the cases Dr. Noyes has investigated have passed into the final stages of depersonalization where they have slipped beyond the confines of this physical reality into something without time or space without the boundaries of a past or a future.

In the third stage the feelings and perceptions are similar to those of people who have experienced clinical death. The out-of-body experiences are also similar.

In an 1892 study, Albert Heim recorded the response of a man who had fallen from a mountain peak.

"I believed myself to be floating downward. Without pain and anxiety I surveyed the situation, the future of my family . . . I cannot think of a milder, finer way to die."

The detached, out-of-body experience is a way of handling the forthcoming death, according to Dr. Noyes.

One person reported that coming close to death was "the most relaxing and joyful experience of my life, and this new place was filled with a light of great brilliance." Others have reported an experience without anxiety, fear, or worries. "I became part of a wonderful bluish sky."

Dr. Noyes tells of a woman who came very near death in an automobile accident.

"My life passed before me in a way that took me back to my childhood. I remembered the smell of pudding my mother used to make."

One man who died for a while after a heart attack told his physicians what it felt like. The doctors, Robert MacMillan and K. W. G. Brown, report that patient's story in the *Canadian Medical Association Journal*.

"The main thing that stands out is the clarity of my thoughts during the episode. Almost immediately I saw myself leave my body, coming out through my head and shoulders. My next sensation was of floating in a bright, pale-yellow light—a very delightful experience."

The experience was so good that the patient later told his doctors, "If I go out again, don't bring me back—it's so beautiful out there." MacMillan and Brown felt that the man's soul might have travelled out of his body.

Those who experience leaving the body have difficulty in describing what they then look like. "I think I was a little like a gray mist." "I had some shape, but not like my body on the bed."

Another view of the Other Side is given from their death beds by persons who do die. Preconceived fears of death are being altered by the visions of stricken persons.

These people have seen a different vision of death.

One dying individual related the following vision seconds before she passed away.

"I see my father coming toward me. I think he wants to take me away with him. Everything there is so beautiful and serene and happy. I am not afraid anymore."

More and more psychiatrists, physicians, priests, and scientists are listening to the reports of dying patients.

Dr. Elisabeth Kubler-Ross is the foremost authority on the subject of death. She is medical director of the Medical Health Center in Flossmoor, Illinois.

In *The Experience of Dying*, Kubler-Ross writes about her grandmother's near-death experience. "She often told my mother that *death* was a peaceful existence, but *dying* was something that people were afraid of."

Dr. Ross wondered why her patients who were so afraid of dying suddenly changed their attitudes. "Why did so few of my patients really fight death at the end?"

It may be that the once-frightened patients have seen the beauty, contentment, and joy that awaits them on the Other Side.

Once a patient gets very near death, fear is not a dominant emotion, reports Dr. Karlis Osis in his monograph, "Deathbed Observations by Doctors and Nurses." They see something just before they die which causes them contentment.

One dying man reported the following:

"I see a bright light . . . It's getting bigger and bigger. It is taking me in. It is warm and good. I . . ." With that the patient died.

In the bestselling book, *Angels*, The Reverend Billy Graham writes: "The Bible guarantees every believer an escorted journey into the presence of Christ by the holy angels."

In *Deathbed Visions* Sir William Barrett quotes the last words of an old woman who was dying.

" 'It's all so dark, I cannot see.' A moment later her face brightened, and she exclaimed: 'Oh, it's lovely and bright; you cannot see as I can.' A little later she said: 'I can see father, he wants me, he is so lonely.' Then, with a rather puzzled expression: 'He has Vida with him.' Turning to her mother—'Vida is with him.' A few moments later she died."

After examining the reports of hundreds of dying people, Dr. Osis verified the existence of deathbed visions and the predominance of images of departed individuals waiting to guide the about-to-be-dead to the Other Side. Osis wrote: "There is something in this type of [vision]which distinctly changes the dying person's outlook on death."

Patients seem to know when their time is up. Any nurse can relate to you story after story of patients who have opened their eyes for a moment and told those around them, "They have come to get me. I'm going now." Soon after, they die. None seem to be frightened with the knowledge that they are going to die.

After interviewing hundreds of people revived from clinical death, Dr. Elisabeth Kubler-Ross has concluded that there is something about the death experience which removes the person's fears of dying.

The visions that come to dying persons are sometimes seen or heard by those gathered around the patient. Proof of the existence of visions from the Other Side may be found in the story told by an Irish priest.

"A history of auditory visions had surrounded this family for hundreds of years. When members of the family came to the final stage in their lives, as they lay on their deathbeds, they would tell those around them that they heard voices."

The priest said, "Once while I was there giving last rites to a very old man, he said to me at the final instant, 'Father, I'm dying, and I hear children crying.'

"It was something that ran through the family's history. I thought it was nothing more than the members carrying through in their hallucinations what they had been told for decades."

If you are told something often enough that something will happen, you get so that you expect it to happen. Even if it does not happen, your subconscious mind makes it seem like it did.

The priest continued, "I didn't think any more about what the old man told me. I assumed that he was hallucinating during his final seconds of life.

"It wasn't until a nun told me what had happened a few years later when she was visiting the family. One of the family was severely hurt in an accident. As he was dying, the nun heard the sound of children crying. There were no children in the house."

When a person faces what he considers to be certain death, after he has stopped resisting death, visions of his past life's experiences flash through his mind; then the person seems to detach from his body. A person who is actually dying sees visions of the Other Side and then seems to detach from the body. The first may be the first part of the journey a person makes to the Other Side. The second may provide a glimpse of the hereafter.

5
A TALK WITH GOD

"In 1959, I caught the Asian flu, and even though I had three little ones to take care of, I ran such a fever that I had to stay in bed. I was the sickest I've ever been. My fever got higher and higher. I hurt and burned all over. I couldn't take care of my family or myself.

"Then I died," said Mary A. of Pennsylvania.

According to the religious teachings of Christianity and Islam, the human soul is judged after death to be fit for either heaven or hell in accordance to the verdict which is based upon the person's best performance while in this life. This view has evolved from Zoroastrianism by way of Pharisaic Judaism. The soul's immortality was something that God judged.

The New Testament presents the next world, the Other Side of this life, as being divided into paradise (or as it is more commonly called, Heaven) and another place where the bad are punished (called Hell).

The Catholic Church refers to a third area, a region

where people go for a temporary cleansing. This place is called purgatory. The woman who caught the Asian flu and temporarily died seemed to have made a journey through something like purgatory. She related the following about her experience while dead:

"I seemed to be able to see myself. I all at once felt myself *soaring up* into space. Faster and faster I went. Space was like a dark void, but it wasn't black. It was more like nothing, nothing at all. I've never been able to find the right words to describe the void in space that I flew through. But it was different from being in a pitch black room. I suppose the only way to get the picture is to actually experience it for yourself. One must die in order to go through what I did.

"The void around death is strange. I didn't feel the passage of time. I only felt that I was moving toward something. What it was I don't know. It was just a feeling I got. There was no sound at all. Total absence of voices, music, or noise. It was the strangest experience I've ever been through. But I liked the feeling."

A belief in an afterlife, whether it is in the form of reincarnation or a heaven and hell, is a matter of faith. One either believes in the sincerity of the person's report and trusts in his observations, or one disregards his stories about journeying to the Other Side and places them in the category of hallucinations. But there have been too many glimpses of the Other Side to label them all the product of a "vivid imagination" and then forget them.

Is the departure of the soul observable? Research scientists, medical doctors, and other experimentally oriented individuals have attempted to verify the existence of the human soul.

The experiences of the clinically dead, reports of individuals involved in near-death accidents, out-of-body travels, and deathbed visions are indications that there is a continuation of something after death.

Dr. Charles Garfield is associated with the University of California's Cancer Research Institute. He told *Newsweek* reporter Kenneth L. Woodward, "I don't take the extreme scientific-materialist position that these are the utterances of deranged persons."

Mary A. believes in the survival of her soul after death. When she died, she flew from her body.

"I saw myself in bed. I remember the brilliant white sheets. I still remember looking down on myself. Then I flew from the room and my dead body on the bed."

As she flew through the void of space toward the unknown, she thought to herself about her family and the responsibilities and obligations she was leaving.

"I was going straight up into outer space when I thought about my three children."

Whether she was able to speak or hear while dead, she does not know, but somehow she managed to get the following thought out: "Please, God, my husband is Protestant and I'm Catholic. Let me live so that I can raise my children as Catholics.' I could see them in their beds."

She pleaded three times and on the third plea, she heard or felt the following: " 'You can stay a little while longer! It is 4:25, and someone else must go in your place!' "

"I then felt this sudden and tremendous smack like a giant slap—my doctor says it was my soul returning to my body."

Mary A. did live. She returned to life to bring up her children as she had promised.

Mary A.'s daughter Connie believes in her mother's journey. "We all felt that Mother was going to die. I have always been psychic, and I knew that Mother was going to die that night. I saw in my mind that she climbed down the stairs on hands and knees to get herself a glass of water. Shortly after she returned to the stairs and got back into bed, I saw her rising from her body on the bed!"

Thus, Connie claims to have psychically sensed the departure of her mother's soul at the instant of death.

"Are you scared of dying now?" I asked Mary A.

"I'm not frightened of death, just the pain that sometimes precedes the final moment. I'm afraid of pain but not of anything after that."

I asked why not.

"Because I found peace, serenity, and joy as I soared in the black void. I remember traveling higher and higher and becoming more and more at peace."

I wondered, "Did you see God or anything that might be the hereafter?"

"No, I only remember a void. I asked God three times for the chance to raise my kids according to certain religious principles. I felt I was in a tunnel, and it was a vivid experience."

When I asked Mary A. what God sounded like, she replied, "He sounded like a loud and powerful drum. His voice vibrated like a drum. I didn't dream it. I had no fear of Him. But I have wondered many times what He meant when He said, 'You can stay a little while longer.' How long is a little while?"

Many people tell of seeing and/or hearing spirits or visions of religious persons. Billy Graham has written about the visions of his dying grandmother. She saw Ben, her late husband, and Jesus Christ. She said, "I see Jesus. He has His arms outstretched toward me. I see Ben, and I see the angels." After telling about what she saw, she died.

Mary A. now plans to move to Florida with her husband who just retired. She reflects, "I sent a prayer to the other person who had to take my place at 4:25. I wonder who it was? . . . I'm not afraid anymore. I felt good as it was happening, and I know the feeling of death."

This kind of experience while clinically dead distinctly changes the person's outlook on life and death. Dr. Karlis Osis described the perceptions of one woman who had died for a while during surgery. She was unconscious for several hours and when she regained consciousness she said she had been on "a high hill like a divide, and she could look down into the Promised Land. She could not describe it well but said it was beautiful, and she was not afraid to cross over [to the Other Side] because it was so beautiful."

The head nurse of one of New York City's largest and most active emergency rooms described her experience with an emergency patient who had been brought in suffering from a massive heart attack. He stated in a very matter-of-fact manner, "I'm going now."

"When he said that, I believed him. Over the years that I have worked in the emergency room, several patients have told me that they were about to die. After making their reports they soon died. The instant before death their faces showed contentment and joy."

Many physicians, nurses, and hospital attendants report

that a conscious dying person is able to recognize and describe his situation. And the view of the hereafer is most pleasant.

In *Rickenbacker: An Autobiography*, Edward V. Rickenbacker describes his glimpse of the Other Side.

"I began to die. I felt the presence of death. I knew that I was going." Rickenbacker knew that he was looking at death close-up. In his deathbed description he reveals the comfort which he found in death.

"You may have heard that dying is unpleasant, but don't you believe it. Dying is the sweetest, tenderest, most sensuous sensation I have ever experienced. Death comes disguised as a sympathetic friend. All was serene; all was calm. How wonderful it would be simply to float out of this world. It is easy to die. You have to fight to live."

6
GOLDEN STREETS
AND PEARLY GATES

"When you die and if you have been good, you will go to heaven. God keeps a file on you all through your life. He knows everything about you—the number of hairs on your head, when you were naughty, and when you were nice; and each of your evil thoughts is recorded for the Final Decision when your name is called out up yonder."

This is a fairly standard story told to a lot of people (mainly children) about what to expect on the Other Side. "If you lead a good life, where your good deeds outweigh your evil deeds, you will enter heaven."

The quality of one's existence after physical death is closely linked to the religious idea that God will keep a record of your deeds in life, judge your performance against standards of good and evil, and send you to either heaven or hell.

The pleasures in the hereafter depend upon one's behavior during the present life. If one is good one could expect to bask in a good afterlife. A bad life transports you into the perpetual horror of hell.

Hell is portrayed as a place where souls go to burn in the eternal fires forever or until the Second Coming, depending on the religious view. Hell is a place to make you wish you had been a better person in this life.

In the Holy Bible, only partial glimpses of heaven and hell are shown. In Luke 12:4-5, people are warned to fear those who can cast you into hell but not those who just kill your body.

"I tell you, my friends, do not fear those who kill the body, and after that have no more that they can do. But I will warn you whom to fear: fear him who, after he has killed, has power to cast into hell; yes, I tell you, fear him!"

In Revelation 12:9, we see that the Devil is a deceiver and the one with the power to kill us and throw us into hell. "And the great dragon was thrown down, that ancient serpent, who is called the Devil and Satan, the deceiver of the whole world—he was thrown down to the earth, and his angels were thrown down with him."

In Matthew 5:22, we find a reference to one characteristic of hell—that of the eternal fires. "But I say to you that everyone who is angry with his brother shall be liable to judgment; whoever insults his brother shall be liable to the council, and whoever says, 'You fool!' shall be liable to the hell of fire." It is commonly thought that sinners must burn in the fires of hell as punishment for their sins.

The story of one woman who experienced death and believed that she saw hell was written down by Jean-Baptiste Delacour in his book *Glimpses of the Beyond*. Janine Eharrat was a ballerina performing on stage when she brushed too near an open flame and caught her clothes on fire. She was taken to a hospital where she died from third-degree burns. Physicians were able to resuscitate her.

Later Janine related her experience in the hereafter.

"I was falling into a deep well. The fall never seemed to end. I was alone in a strange and unfamiliar world surrounded by huge licking flames. The flames got bigger, and their incandescent redness became so glaring that I thought I would perish of fear.

"It really and truly had to be hell!

"The thick curtain of fire had to be the devil's work, for how else were the leaping flames being fed? They seemed to be coming in a wild dance out of the interior of the earth, their bizarre shapes constantly changing. The ground under me was incandescent, a lavalike, boiling mud."

Janine went on to tell how she met her departed grandmother who showed her the book of the dead where one's past is kept.

In Matthew 5:29, we find another reference to hell. "If your right eye causes you sin, pluck it out and throw it away; it is better that you lose one of your members than your whole body be thrown into hell."

Another woman who "died" during an operation has told about her visit to hell.

"I found myself (perhaps just my soul) completely alone in a place of extreme brightness. Everything was a brilliant white like the sun shining on cliffs of stone or ice. A single large eye looked on me in a searching manner. The eye, that could have been swimming around, had lashes and a brow so that I recognized it as my own. It was searching me out and I asked it what I had done to be sent to hell. Then a thought replied, 'no big thing, just a lot of small ones.' I was not visible. I don't know if my body was there or not, but I was certain of spending eternity in a place of glaring whiteness completely alone with an eye searching my life forever. This was hell."

This report is in "depersonalization in the Face of Life-Threatening Danger," an article by Dr. Russell Noyes and Mr. LeRoy Kletti to appear in *Omega*.

The picture painted seems to make all the earthly abstinence worthwhile. Good times are to be had once one is allowed to pass St. Peter on the way through the Pearly Gates. Inside the Kingdom of Heaven, you can expect the very best, according to some people. The streets and buildings are paved with gold. Silver and other precious metals are to be found everywhere. The Kingdom of Heaven shines with a brilliant radiance. Everywhere the multitudes are singing the joys of salvation to God. Angels are everywhere. It is definitely a place of good and beauty.

A view of the Other Side is found in the Revised Standard Version of the *Holy Bible*. In Revelation 21:21, heaven is described. "And the twelve gates were twelve pearls, each of the gates made of a single pearl, and the street of the city was pure gold, transparent as glass."

We get a very pretty picture of the hereafter by reading the Bible. But is it what we will actually find when we make that long journey to the Other Side? Very few of the people who have returned from the hereafter have reported seeing earthlike objects, and none have seen golden streets and pearly gates. Is the Bible wrong? Or have those who have been clinically dead just been hallucinating about the Other Side?

There are 13 million Southern Baptists in all the 50 states. They believe in a personal commitment to Christ, and they believe that the Bible is infallible.

I talked to the Reverend Jaroy Weber, the outgoing president of the Southern Baptist Convention, to learn if his reading of the Bible had led him to believe in golden streets and pearly gates. Reverend Weber answered, "The use of the word 'gold' in Revelation is only an indicator of the great things that we will expect when we arrive there after physical death. The value to be found in heaven will transcend earthly riches."

In *Angels*, Billy Graham, who is the standard-bearer for the Southern Baptists and their foremost evangelist, told about a dying Chinese who had exclaimed on his deathbed, "I see Jesus standing at the right hand of God, and [my daughter] is with him."

Reverend Weber went on to describe his opinion of deathbed visions. " 'I can see Christ coming for me,' is commonly reported by dying persons who are devoutly religious. This may be some proof of the existence of the hereafter. Someone who really wants to see Jesus may hallucinate a vision of Him in the final moment of intense suffering. Since very few dying persons have reported seeing the Lord in their final moments, deathbed visions reflect a common experience and not their imaginations."

Devoutly religious persons who have nearly died, or who have been clinically dead, rarely report experiences containing descriptions of streets of gold, pearly gates, angels, or any of the other things one might expect religious people to see.

"I was standing off on the side watching them attempt

41

to get me alive. I hoped they would leave me alone," said a sixty-five-year old man who was clinically dead and quickly resuscitated.

A nurse said, "He was dead as a doornail. The doctor gave him ninety-nine electric shocks before they got his heart to beat again on its own. I've never heard of so many shocks being administered to anyone before. But he did live for three months after the procedures were administered in [the intensive care unit]."

The man later said of his experience of being dead, "I remember rising from [the Intensive Care Unit] in a mist or cloud. I went faster and faster. I went through a void. It had no color. I don't think it was black, but the void had nothing in it except a pinpoint of light far away which I seemed to be heading toward at a rapid speed."

The first thing that I was aware of was moving very rapidly down this endless tunnel. There was a bright light at the end of it. I sort of felt like I was in a low sports car doing about 120 miles an hour. Then I came to a light.

"The pinpoint of light grew larger, and I went into it. I know I entered Heaven. It felt good to be there. No worries or pain. I felt the presence of another being, but I never saw anyone. I just had a great feeling of joy and happiness. Then I was pulled out of this paradise, and I seemed to snap back into my body in Intensive Care . . .

"I guess it was the work of the physicians that got me back. I did not want to come back."

One reoccurring thought that worried the man after he got out of the hospital was, "The place I went to felt good enough to be a heaven, but there weren't any gold or riches to be found there."

As Jaroy Weber pointed out, the Bible's mention of golden streets and pearly gates does not mean that that is literally what we can expect to find on the Other Side. Words can never describe what must be experienced to be understood. Reverend Weber concluded with the thought that "words alone are incapable of adequately describing the greatness and richness that one will find in heaven."

The Southern Baptist Convention is Protestantism's largest denomination. Most members are "born again" Christians who have had an emotional experience which caused a religious change and brought about a "new life."

Being "born again" causes an awareness and transformation in the individual almost identical to the awareness of those experiencing clinical death, a near-death situation, or deathbed visions. All cause profound changes in the individuals. For the Southern Baptists, as well as other religions, God, the hereafter, and other aspects of the Other Side, are revealed through the Bible.

Jimmy Carter said, in an interview for *U.S. News and World Report*, July 19, 1976, that he profoundly felt the presence of the Holy Spirit. "Since then, I've had an inner peace and inner conviction and assurance that transformed my life for the better."

Thus, a Christian knows that this is the truth because he takes a leap of faith with his belief in God.

While the vast majority of the people I interviewed concerning their visits to the Other Side were happy with what they had experienced, some people returned filled with horror and displeasure. Some thought that they had visited hell and had been lucky enough to be brought back to this life. Some did not have a good recollection of their time while dead, yet something affected their subconscious minds negatively, and it has stayed with them.

C.E. Green, in "Analysis of Spontaneous Cases" (published in *Proceedings of the Society for Psychic Research, 1960*), writes about one woman's experience in the hereafter: "When I got up with the intention of getting back into bed to my surprise and a feeling of *horror*, I saw my own body stretched on the bed asleep—at any rate completely motionless . . . I was compressed back into that body as a picture in its frame . . . When I had recovered my composure I could think of no rational explanation of what had occurred, but I went over each impression and movement very carefully . . ." For years after the occurrence, the negative feeling was not easily forgotten.

One woman I interviewed felt depressed after her experience while clinically dead. She remembered only fragments of things concerning what happened while she was dead, but she came out of the experience feeling much worse than before she had died.

"It happened five years ago. It was in 1971 when the doctors had missed their diagnosis and had given me the wrong treatments. I suffered a severe reaction to their treatments, and I died for a moment. They worked on me to get my heart started or something like that. I felt everything become black, and I was very much alone in a nothing. I saw nothing, I heard nothing. Before I had this experience with death, I did not believe in God. After dying and experiencing what I did, I changed my mind."

"What did you experience besides the nothing?" I asked.

"I don't know exactly. I felt that there was something out there waiting for me. Friends have told me about feeling the presence of evil spirits. I think that is what I felt. I can't tell you what it looked like, or anything about it. I just know that it was there in the dark with me. It was a horrible feeling. I felt nothing else but it.''

I wondered how she had felt since the experience.

''I wanted to have children, but I don't seem to be able to have any. During the past two years, I have started to have anxiety attacks which have been getting worse and worse. I can't work any longer. I am in pain from severe neuritis. I used to be happy, now I am constantly thinking about death and that thing that is waiting out there for me.

''It's strange that after these five years I still dream at night about dying. Now, whenever I am happy doing something, I sort of die. My friends were telling me last week that while I was playing and having fun at the piano, a deathlike pall came over my face. They thought I had died.

''Sometimes I think that I'm the reincarnated spirit of my dead sister who mother liked more than me.''

Why this woman had such bad experiences on the Other Side is not known. She hadn't tried to kill herself, nor had she lived a bad life. Perhaps she only thought she died and what she experienced was only a bad reaction to the drugs she had been given.

Regardless of why she had a painful reaction to her experience, her vision is definitely a rarity. Most people are filled with joy and wonderment after their journeys to the Other Side.

7
THE OTHER BODY

One of the phenomena perceived by a clinically dead person is a feeling of detachment, a separation from his body. In almost every instance where an individual has died and then been resuscitated, individuals have reported traveling out of their physical body and continuing their existence in an almost spiritlike body. These traveling episodes have been called "out-of-body experiences" (usually are abbreviated as "OOBE" in scientific literature). In many cases OOBE's have been experimentally proven to the satisfaction of once-skeptical scientists.

Out-of-body experiences of clinically dead patients have been construed to be another view and glimpse of the Other Side. H. H. Price, in his article "What Kind of Next World?", written for Arnold Toynbee's *Man's Concern with Death*, describes the relationship between OOBE's and the Other Side. He believes that one's experiences here travel to the Other Side when death occurs. An afterlife means consciousness and life experiences. "In this way, the idea of life after death is closely bound up with the idea of 'the Next World' or the 'Other World.' This Other World is what the surviving person is supposed to be conscious of."

Price believes that everyone has a soul or spirit. "Each of us does in fact possess such a 'higher' body even in this present life, and this is the explanation of what are called 'out-of-the-body experiences (experiences of being out of the physical body)."

The concept of spiritual survival is another view of the Other Side. This consists of thoughts, memories, and consciousness. While the person is alive and not threatened with the prospect of a certain and impending death, or the person is on his deathbed and knows that he will die within a few seconds, individuals continually try to interact with the physical environment. It is interaction and integration with this reality which creates the inability to perceive the Other Side.

There are still other ways to reach the Other Side and see what it is like. Indian members of the Native American Church have religious experiences while they chew on the buds of the peyote cactus plant. While engaging in the religious ceremony an altered state of awareness allows them to "see" the Other Side through visions. The Indians' visions are similar to those of a dying man—visions of departed loved ones coming to get him and escort him to the Other Side.

It appears that if we are to "see" the Other Side, we must alter our conscious states of awareness (either through death itself, through drugs, or through the experience of near and almost certain death) to remove the shackles brought on by the physical reality of this world.

A person's physical interactions cease at death. A person's soul continues onward even though the physical body has died. The soul is free to roam at will across the vastness of the spiritual universe once the shackles are removed by death.

Persons who come close to death or who have experienced death briefly frequently change their attitudes toward death and are no longer frightened by it. Some even wish to return to the death state. One revived woman said, "I didn't want to come back. Death is nice. Now I want to die again, and I'm not scared of dying."

Abraham Maslow, a social psychologist who has made a lifetime study of "life" and "death," writes in *Religions, Values and Peak-Experiences* that something happens to people who have brushed close to death which causes them to perceive the Other Side differently. Maslow uses the term "sweet death" to describe that mystical experience in the clinical death or near-death experience which removes a person's fear of the Other Side.

One well-known radio announcer had reported several out-of-body experiences while sleeping. His spirit leaves his body and goes to the roof of the building where it is confronted by a being which is similar in appearance, but with a totally evil spirit.

Other out-of-body experiences where people have become detached from themselves and come face to face with their "twin" beings have been documented by Dr. N. Lukianowica in the *Archives of Neurology and Psychiatry*. The person's double confuses the person by mimicking all the original person's characteristics—his style of walking, his smiles and laughter, mannerisms in talking, and so on. During their OOBE's, these people believe that they are more alive than when they were in their physical bodies. Dr. Lukianowica calls the phenomena of OOBE and the seeing of one's self as "autoscopic phantom hallucination." To the participating individual, this so-called hallucination is *real*.

A thirty-four-year-old businessman, a very sane, normal, and otherwise rational citizen, has described an out-of-body experience that occurred when he was eight years old. At first his OOBE's were frightening to him because he thought that he was losing his mind. Now he more or less accepts the OOBE's and does not worry about them.

"The first time it happened . . . the first time I felt my mind leave my body . . . I was a little frightened. I was eight years old. It was around eight o'clock at night, and I was home wishing that I could be at my best friend's house where he was having his birthday party. My Mother had kept me home that night since I had gotten sick and was running a little fever. I was mad, and I kept thinking to myself over and over, 'I wish I was there. I wish I was there.' My friend lived on Main Street, about five blocks away. I could picture the house and in my imagination I saw a vision of the party and the fun everyone must have been having. Then a strange thing happened. I was still thinking hard about the party I was missing when I felt wide awake. I did not have a fever anymore. All at once I drifted out of my body. I remember the weightless feeling. I felt free of restrictions. I remember the events vividly. I had to look down to see the little boy's body lying there on the bed, and I knew at once it was my body! I don't remember if it was breathing. It did look lifeless, almost dead. I drifted up toward the ceiling like a balloon. I floated there for a moment. There was a difference between my floating and my dreaming. I was not dreaming at this time.

"After floating near the ceiling for a moment, I decided to see if I could control my floating movements. I don't know how I did it, but I could float from one corner of the room to the next. I thought about my friend's party, and I suddenly found myself going through my door—not opening it, but through it! The next thing that I knew I was drifting toward the front door of my friend's house. I went through the door the same way that I went through my door at home. Everyone there was really having a good time. My friend was there, and I tried getting his attention by calling out to him. "How's it going, Jim? I thought I'd drop by for your party.' But he did not hear me nor did he see me. I could see everybody who was there, including some people I'd never seen before. I heard Jim talking to one stranger. 'I have seen you before at school, but I didn't know that we were neighbors.' The stranger answered, 'We only moved in last month from Dallas, and I don't get out much. I'm Alan.'

"The conversation continued, but I lost interest and drifted around the room catching parts of other things. No one knew that I was there. I was lonely and decided to go back to my own house. For a while I did not know how to get out of Jim's house. I was scared and nobody seemed to care. The people at the party were not aware of my distress. I drifted around the room for a time. What was amazing was that after a while I started to play games with the people and objects in the room. I found I could drift through the people! I was transparent to them, and I went right through the people in the room.

"I still wanted to get back home. Then I heard a voice

calling from a great distance, 'Ralph, Ralph, wake up.' The voice was worried, and I suddenly realized that it belonged to my Mother. Instantly I was back in my body lying on the bed in my house. 'What do you want?' I asked my Mother. 'I thought that you were dead for a moment,' she said. She gave me some pills and stayed near me for a while. 'The journey to my friend's house must have been a dream,' I thought to myself before falling to sleep.

"It was a week later at school that I was talking to my friend Jim. I told him about the party and said, 'I dreamed that you were talking to this new guy, and he was telling you that he had just moved into the neighborhood from Dallas. He didn't get to go out much and that was the reason that you didn't know that he was your neighbor.'

"Jim was a little startled at first because he said that that was right, 'How did you know?' I told him that I thought that I had traveled there with my mind. My friend thought someone who was at the party told me about Alan. But this wasn't true. No one told me about anything that happened at the party. I had not spoken to anyone before meeting Jim at school. I was embarrassed that he didn't believe me and I decided to go along with his guess that I had talked to someone.

"I haven't talked to anyone about this since. This feeling of traveling out of my body has occurred three times since. None of which to the extent of the first time. These travels have always been very pleasurable, but I'm still scared that I am *losing* my mind."

The spontaneous detachment of the soul from an otherwise healthy individual is commonly reported in the literature. A lengthy and vivid account of an OOBE is presented in William Gerhardi's book *Resurrection*. In the introduction to his book, Gerhardi tells his reader that "incredible as it may seem," the experience which is so eloquently described is "a true experience." He also reports that he took no drugs or anything else which would have caused him to lose a portion of his mind to insanity and hallucination and brought on his feeling of traveling outside his body.

Gerhardi's first experience with being out his body occurred one night as he was dreaming about pulling a tooth. He was lying in bed in the dark. He remembers reaching out his hand to turn on the bedside light. The light had been in the same place for a long time and in the past Gerhardi had always been able to locate the light in the dark, but on the particular night his arm and fingers felt nothing but a void. Suddenly he became very wide awake and conscious of the fact that he was floating away from his bed and suspended above his own body.

"To my utter astonishment that broad cable of light at the back of me illuminated the face on the pillow, as if attached to the brow of the sleeper. The sleeper was myself, not dead, but breathing peacefully, my mouth slightly open . . ., and here was I, outside it, watching it with a thrill of joy and fear. There was this uncanny tape of light between us like an umbilical cord, by means of which the body on the bed was kept breathing while its mould wandered about the flat through space which seemed as dense as water."

Gerhardi felt like he was moving through an unsteady, thick sea which moved him about in it. He was completely conscious. He felt more alive than when he was within his body. He was not dead.

Gerhardi could fly through the front door. "Now I could fly to New York, visit a friend, if I liked, and it wouldn't take me a moment."

A dream? Gerhardi thought not since he was able to detach himself from the body almost at will and the process happened several times in varying circumstances. The real reason that he did not think that he was dreaming about floating away from his body was that he could relate stories about intimate things that his friends were doing in the privacy of their homes, miles away. They were, needless to say, very surprised by his habit of popping in on them, unannounced.

Rosalind Heywood writes, in "Attitudes to Death in the Light of Dreams and Other 'Out-of-the-body' Experiences" (In Toynbee's *Man's Concern with Death*), that it is difficult to understand the feelings of people "whose attitude to death has been changed by what they believe to be OOBE." Leaving one's physical body changes one's feeling toward the world.

Some researchers feel that individuals who report out-of-body experiences may be dreaming, hallucinating, or making up the stories for personal attention. A group of scientifically oriented researchers called parapsychologists have been investigating out-of-body experiences for insights into areas such as astral projection, telepathic communications, and reincarnation. Now once skeptical scientists are beginning to reconsider the facts which support the theory that there is indeed a soul that can leave the physical body.

Out-of-body experiences are almost exactly like the experiences of those who have been clinically dead for a period of time. Victor Solow, who was dead for many minutes, reported the feeling of sudden departure from his physical body and a traveling sensation as he approached and finally touched and became part of a giant pulsating grid.

Emergency rooms are a source of similar stories. A patient who has been pronounced dead suddenly finds himself in a long tunnel. He is rushing toward something in the distance while a loud noise rings in his ears. Then everything becomes quieter, and the patient finds himself watching emergency room personnel attempting to resuscitate him. Later, the patient is able to repeat what was said and describe the procedures that were used on him to bring him back to life. A being in the form of a light comes to serve as a guide to the Other Side. Dead friends and relatives gather to communicate in a nonverbal manner. The individual reviews his past life in a panoramic vision. He sees his life pass before him as it would at a movie. Reluctantly, the person returns to his body as he is pulled out of this other realm by the resuscitation process.

A woman who had experienced a very difficult delivery of a baby girl had a vivid recollection of the detachment of her self from the physical body. The woman had lost a lot of blood during the delivery. The woman died. There was no blood pressure and her breathing ceased. Quick-thinking doctors were able to resuscitate her. Later she told about her feelings while clinically dead.

"For a second everything went totally black. Not really black like the color, but a voidlike black. I heard loud noises that seemed to rush by me. They were so loud that they were painful. I knew I was moving. Something

54

jerked me out of my body. I was carried, or pushed, through this long tunnel, and I suddenly came to a crevice that fell away to such a distance that everything looked black.

"I saw a strange light in the distance that was kind of like a glob of light. It was indistinct. I think that something or somebody was in that glob of light. A bright cloud enveloped me for an instant, then I was pulled out of the cloud, and I found myself floating near the corner of the roof where the two walls came together. I found myself in the delivery room watching from a distance their attempts to bring me back to life. The body on the white table —deathly white—it was me!

"There was my body on the bed and here I was floating above it watching the whole thing like it was a movie. It was very real. I could actually float through the wall of the delivery room, and I drifted down the halls of the hospital. I don't know what I looked like for sure. I think I was a transparent cloud but regardless of my looks, no one seemed to notice that I was gliding through the air near them. I suppose that I was invisible to them although I could see and hear them very well.

"I came back to the delivery room. There seemed to be something pulling me back to my body. The entire experience of floating out of my body was very good. It may seem strange but I really did not want to join with that body on the table. But I was jerked very forcefully to it. I remember something about reentering it. After that I can't remember a thing until I came to hours later in my bed in an intensive care unit. I did not feel good, but over the next few days I did get better. That was twenty-five years ago. I remember the incident well. It stands out in my mind as clear as anything I see now. I know that I died and I would like to do it again. It was very pleasant.''

In an address to the Royal Medical Society in Edinburgh in 1937, Lord Geddes, a professor and physician, described an account of an individual who died for a brief while and then was revived.

''I suddenly realized that my consciousness was separating from another consciousness which was also me. . . . Gradually I realized that I could see not only my body and the bed in which it was, but everything in the whole house and garden, and then I realized that I was not only seeing 'things' at home, but in London and in Scotland, in fact wherever my attention was directed . . . I was free in a time dimension of space, wherein 'now' was in some way equivalent to 'here' in the ordinary three dimensional space of everyday life. I next realized that my vision included not only 'things' in the ordinary three dimensional places that I was in. Although I had no body, I had what appeared to be perfect two-eyed vision, and what I saw can only be described in this way, that I was conscious of a psychic stream flowing with life through time, and this gave me the impression of being visible, and it seemed to me to have a particularly intense iridescence.''

Dr. Geddes's out-of-body experience, like that of the woman in delivery, occurred as the result of clinical death. The following, strikingly similar, incident occurred to a perfectly fit mountain climber who thought he was about to die after falling over the edge of a cliff.

''I found myself hanging on the rope a few feet below the crest of the ridge. During the time I was doing this a curious rigidity or tension gripped my whole being, mental and physical . . . It was outside my experience. It was as though all life's forces were in process of undergoing some fundamental evolutionary change, the change called death . . . I know now that death is not to be feared. Time no longer existed as time . . . Then suddenly this feeling was superseded by a feeling of complete indifference and detachment, detachment as to what was happening or likely to happen to that body. I seemed to stand outside my body. I, that is, my consciousness, was apart from my body and not in the least concerned with what was befalling it.'' (From F. S. Smythe, *The Spirit of the Hills.*)

The experience of leaving the body seems to be a pleasurable thing regardless of whether one does it spontaneously from a healthy body, or as a form of flight from a body in pain, or as the result of being clinically dead.

Out-of-body experiences are offering skeptical scientists proof of the existence of a human spirit or soul. The constraints which shackle our perceptions to this reality are released when our spirits travel out of our bodies. Altered states of consciousness allow individuals to report on their views of the Other Side.

8
THE BEAUTIFUL OTHER SIDE

"I was shot in the stomach with a .45 caliber pistol. It entered from the front and went all the way through me. It just missed my spinal column."

I asked Vivian if she remembered anything about the feeling of being shot with such a very powerful gun.

"I heard the loud explosion and at the same time I was thrown backwards by a very powerful force. I don't remember crashing against a wall. I can't remember falling to the floor."

I remembered my first night that I worked in the emergency room of a Texas hospital. The police and ambulance personnel had brought in a gunshot victim from one of the late night beer halls.

They took the man from the stretcher and placed him on the examination table of the emergency room. The man had seven bullet holes in various parts of his body. There were three bullet holes in his groin. Later I found out that this man in the emergency room had been dancing with another man's woman. A gun was pulled. Six shots were fired. The man reloaded and fired an additional two shots into his wife s dancing partner. None of the bullets were fatal.

We did not give the man any pain killers. There were two reasons for this. Number one—the man had been drinking and it might have killed him to sedate him. Number two—he was not in any pain. The only time during his stay in the emergency room that he got excited and felt pain was when we catherized him. Even though his bladder and kidneys were punctured by the bullets, he did not want that tube inserted into his body.

All in all, the man was extremely lucky. The man that shot him had used a .22 caliber, "Saturday Night" special. The bullets were small and the man's aim was terrible.

During the five hours that the man was in the emergency room, I had ample time to talk to him about the shooting.

He would not tell the police who shot him, but he told me in private, "I know who did it. When I'm out of here in a few weeks, my brothers and I will make sure justice is done."

I can never be sure if the man lived up to his announcement, but I would guess that one of the men who came into the emergency room during the next six months was the receiver of the personal "justice" of the victim of eight gunshot wounds.

But the woman I was now interviewing had been shot with a much more powerful weapon. A Marine Corps friend who knew handguns once told me that a .45 could do great damage to a human body by just grazing it.

I asked her about the feelings that raced through her mind after being shot.

"I thought I was sinking into a dark, dark space. A void. It wasn't black, just void of color."

"Were you frightened when you didn't see anything around you?"

"No. I suddenly felt great peace. Maybe it was a wave of bliss or happiness that came over me."

"Any pain?"

"None at all. I had nothing on my mind except that contented, peaceful feeling."

The incident occurred in New York more than eleven years ago. Her five year old son witnessed the accident.

"The doctors told me it was a miracle that I was brought back to life. They pronounced me DOA —dead-on-arrival to Coney Island Hospital.

"One of the doctors at the emergency room said when the ambulance brought me to the hospital, 'Why waste our time. She's dead.' "

"You were completely gone when they got you to the hospital?"

"That's right. It was lucky for me that one of the doctors decided that he would try to save me. He felt that I was too young to die."

"How old were you when the shooting took place?"

"I was twenty-three years old."

She did feel a lot of pain from the gunshot, but this was after the operations to revive her. While she was dead on the table in the emergency room, she felt complete bliss. She was at peace with herself.

"I suffered for years after the shooting, but during the time they were trying to bring me back from the other side I felt happiness and contentment."

Vivian drifted from her tormented body and entered the

peaceful bliss that many think await us when our physical bodies die.

"I could still perceive my body, but in a strange way. It is awful hard to explain how I felt while I was dead. I knew that my body was in tremendous pain, but I didn't feel it. I thank God that I did not have to suffer."

I was curious about the lasting effects on the personality of an individual who has died, whose spirit has departed the physical body, and then is pulled back to live once again.

"Did the experience of dying change your view toward God?"

"Yes. Before dying I didn't put much faith in religious things. Now I know there is a hereafter. I know there is a God. I don't care what skeptics say. I know what I felt while I was dead."

I asked, "Did the fact that you died and were brought back change your feelings about life?"

"I am much more mystical. I feel things that others don't seem to have the capacity to do so."

"Like what?"

"One Saturday morning five years ago I suddenly woke up and said to my husband: 'There is something wrong. What time is it?' "

"He told me it was 5:30 A.M., and he wanted to know what was wrong. I said I really couldn't say. I just had this feeling of impending disaster. We found out later that Pop had had a heart attack at 5:30 that morning and he later died."

I felt kind of strange talking to someone who could foresee the future and talk about impending deaths. I asked her to elaborate more on her death experiences.

"While I was dead I felt myself drifting away, further and further away. I drifted and drifted. Then I remembered seeing myself smiling. I was looking back at my physical body and I was seeing myself smiling."

"Could you see anything around you?"

"Everything was dark. All darkness and completely black. Except that I could see myself smiling because I was contented and happy."

"Are you afraid of dying now since your experience with death eleven years ago?"

"I'm not afraid of death anymore. I used to be terribly frightened of the dark and of dying. Once I saw how nice it is to die, my fears left and never returned."

Vivian described how the doctors had worked over her body for seven hours before they repaired the damage done by the bullet. They made an incision from her breasts down six inches past her navel. They spread the rib cage apart and reached in with their hands and massaged her heart. They injected adrenaline directly into the heart. Finally the heart started to beat, feebly at first, then gradually it gained its strength. Then for several hours the team of physicians in the operating room repaired the damage done by the huge bullet.

"The doctor that brought me back to life later came to my hospital room and talked to me about his life-saving skills."

"He told me, 'An artist feels a great deal of satisfaction when he completes a long and difficult painting. A painter recognizes his greatest achievement. You, Vivian, are my masterpiece! I just knew that I couldn't let you lay there without trying to bring you back to life.'"

The doctor was right. He had performed more than a masterpiece. He had performed a miracle.

"The doctor saved my life. When I got to the hospital I was dead, and he refused to let me stay dead. I am so very happy that he did what he did."

"I rarely talk about my experiences with death because some people don't believe that I experienced something wonderful on the operating table while I was dead."

I questioned her about her attitude toward heaven and hell since she is one of the few that has seen the Other Side and lived to tell about it.

"It is not so much what I saw, as what I felt while I was dead that causes me to believe in the hereafter. I believe in hell on earth. When I was dead and the bullet had gone through my stomach tearing its way through a large vein, I was shown a beautiful thing. I found my God."

Several times during my talk with Vivian, she stressed that she was not making anything up. She was especially concerned that I wouldn't believe her experiences. But she need not worry, for her husband supports her. The hospital confirms it and her attending physician agrees.

"Death is a beautiful experience. It is not scary nor frightening. I am ready to die at any time for I have made peace with my God."

Vivian is not the only person who has died and has been faced with a pleasant journey to the Other Side. During December of 1976, I was in Hobbs, New Mexico, a small town near the Texas border. I was granted an interview for my book with a woman on the condition that I not use her name. She was somewhat apprehensive that her friends would think she was senile.

"I was at the Mayo Clinic in 1949 having surgery when the doctors noticed that I suddenly had no pulse or respiration. The doctors immediately brought me back to life."

"Did you feel anything while you were dead?"

''Yes, just before I died I felt a lot of pain. Then it went away.''

''What happened to you while you were dead?''

''I felt myself float out of my body. I swear to you that I pulled out of my body and floated up into the air over my body below.''

''Could you hear or see anything?''

''I saw myself on the table below. I heard the doctors talking to one another: 'She's gone!' And I knew that they were pronouncing me dead.''

''Did it scare you that you were dead?''

''No. I felt good. It sounds strange, but it was a relief to be dead. I felt no pain. I just floated up near the ceiling watching the activities below. I really did not think about anything. I just floated up there.''

The doctors started their life saving techniques oblivious to the floating spirit above them.

''I never felt so good as while I was dead. I had felt pain for such a long time, then it vanished and I suddenly felt rosy all over.''

''Do you think that you got to see the hereafter while you were dead?''

''Something very strange and at the same time very beautiful occurred while I was out of my body. There was something in the distance which looked beautiful and I felt I was being slowly pulled toward it. I think that if the doctors hadn't been successful in bringing me back to life, I would have discovered what the beautiful thing was. I don't know what it was out there, but I know it was the most beautiful and peaceful thing I have ever seen.''

''Are you scared of death?''

''Only in dying a slow death. I am afraid of having

death drawn out. I don't want to be kept alive with a machine. I'm almost eighty years old and I'm ready to go at any time God wants me.''

I talked with a man who, as a result of being involved in a disastrous automobile accident, was left a handicapped person for the rest of his life. He is confined to a bed because he cannot walk.

''I was driving home one evening. It was a nice time of the day. The sun was just starting to sink below the horizon. I was not paying a lot of attention to my driving. I had been over this road many times before. I must have been thinking about the girl I was going to take out later that evening.''

''There was a car coming toward the intersection, but since the stop sign was for the driver of that car I assumed that he would heed the sign and stop. He didn't.''

''My car crashed into the other car and I spun around the intersection. Later we were to find out that the impact severed the brake lines and broke the steering mechanism. I had no control over the car after the initial impact. I became a passive viewer of the whole train of things. It was like watching a slow motion picture show. I felt like I was detached from my body and from the car. I felt like everything was going by me very slowly. I didn't get excited or anything. I just watched the events take place. I knew that the sheet metal on the car was being ripped off, that the glass was breaking around me, and that the car's frame was being bent around a tree. It didn't matter because I was watching it from a distance. I think that I was floating above the accident.''

''Then I felt myself die. Suddenly I knew I was in heaven. Heaven was green in color. It was like a fresh, cool valley just after a Spring-time shower has passed over.''

"What else did you see?"

"A cross."

"Are you religious?"

"Before the accident—No. After—yes!"

"Why the sudden transformation?"

"I saw Jesus on the cross. He didn't want me to stay there in heaven. Jesus kicked me out of Heaven."

I was somewhat shocked. I thought that the man was trying to put a story over on me. I talked to his nurses, his friends, his physicians. While they could not swear that the man saw and talked to Jesus while he was dead, they do not think that he is playing a practical joke. He did die in an automobile accident and had to be resuscitated eight times in all before the ambulance got him to the hospital.

"I don't remember anything about the seven deaths that I had on the way to the hospital in the ambulance. I only remember that I died. I was surely in what I saw as heaven. And I did see Jesus, His blood, and a cross."

Maybe the sudden shock and trauma of the automobile accident caused him to hallucinate. In fact, that argument could be presented for any of the cases in which a person claims to have experiences on the Other Side.

Margret M's father died two times, once in 1945, and again, permanently in 1960. Mr. L. was visiting his daughter's home in New York in 1945, when he suffered severe chest pains. It was three a.m. when the doctor arrived at the home. Mr. L. suffered a heart attack and died in the presence of his daughter and the physician. The doctor pronounced Mr. L. dead and pulled the sheet over the dead man's head.

But on an impulse the doctor pulled the sheet back and asked Margret: "Do you have an eyedropper and some whiskey?"

Margret told me, "We placed a few drops of the whiskey on the back of Mr. L's tongue."

"My dad did not swallow or do anything else. He did not breathe. He did not have a heart beat. He was very dead."

"The physician told me, 'I really think that this is it for your dad."

But Margret and the physician waited by the body to see if the whiskey would have any effect on the dead body. Something kept telling the daughter and the doctor to wait and to take their time. There weren't any vital signs at all, but still they hesitated in covering the body with the sheet again.

The doctor told Margret, "Let me try it one more time."

The doctor listened to the body with the stethoscope and he heard nothing indicating life.

I asked Margret if they used any mechanical or electrical methods to get the heart going again. They did nothing.

As he listened again his eyes brightened and he told Margret, "I hear something."

"Faintly, very faintly at first, the heart started beating on its own. It increased in strength and my dad returned from the land of the dead."

I asked Margret what her father told her about the Other Side.

"After my father got his strength back within an hour, he couldn't wait to tell us in very emotional terms what he had experienced while he was dead."

"My father was always very calm and not given to great amounts of emotional feelings, but on this occasion he was in an entirely novel mood. He was very excited about what had happened to him while he was dead."

Mr. L. told Margret the following story about his experiences while he was dead:

"I knew that I was dead. I heard things that suddenly became beautiful music. I heard the most beautiful music I have ever heard played. That pain in my chest vanished and I started to float up and away from my body. I felt myself going, going, going away. And I was being accompanied by beautiful music."

I thought it was pretty strange for a dead man to be hearing music until I read Scott Rogo's article called "Some 'Musical' Out-of-the-Body Experiences," in *Parapsychology Review*, (January-February, 1975). Mr. Rogo described several instances of individuals having out-of-body experiences and hearing music. In natural cases where the individual is faced with illness, near death, or in normal health, the music that is reported being heard is described in terms of beauty. Music heard during enforced incidents (suffocations, drowning, deliberate attempts at projection or out-of-body travels, hypnosis) is described as being more flat.

Margret's father, Mr. L., heard music as he felt himself leave the body. He did not see anything, he only heard music.

Margret said, "My father told us, 'I saw nothing. I think that I was in a dark void, but I could feel myself floating above my body.'"

"My dad was never frightened of death after his experience."

Mr. L. said to Margret once after he had died and returned, " 'I wish I was back there listening to that beautiful music. I did not want to come back to life.' "

Death may be the greatest experience in one's existence according to some of those that have been to the Other Side and have returned.

9
EVIDENCE OF A SOUL

Scientists are now convinced that the human soul continues to exist after the death of the physical body. Reports given by people who have been clinically dead supply part of the proof.

In 1975 a woman was brought into the emergency room of a hospital. She had suffered a heart attack on the streets of New York, near the Empire State Building. She died enroute to this hospital and was dead for about two minutes before they were able to get her heart and respiration going again. Throughout the entire period, from the moment she felt herself die to the point at which they resuscitated her, the woman was aware of the events around her. But she did not think that what she felt was the same as when she perceived things through her physical senses. It was as though a new spirit perceived another realm of existence which was parallel to physical reality.

"I suddenly felt weightless as though I had become a cloud. I drifted up and out of my body. I suddenly became transported through space and time at great speed. I saw glowing clouds of light around me that contained spirits of others. I could look down and see the doctors working on me in the emergency room. I watched with a detached interest their hurried efforts to attach things to my body.''

Reports made by individuals who have experienced spontaneous out-of-body detachments bear striking similarities to the reports of individuals who had left their bodies when they experienced clinical death. Both groups describe floating out of the body, watching events occurring below them, seeing their bodies, traveling to other geographic areas and to other dimensions of time and place, and an ability to pass through walls.

Logic dictates that if there actually is a human soul or spirit, its continued existence must be shown through the phenomena described as out-of-body experiences. Religious teachings contain many references to the transcendental qualities of the human soul or spirit which continues in its existence even after the physical body has ceased to live.

Immortality and everlasting life for the human *spirit* is promised in the Holy Bible. In Matthew 10:26-28, the separation of mind and body is revealed. Jesus, in instructing his twelve disciples, said, '' 'So have no fear of them; for nothing is covered that will not be revealed, or hidden that will not be known. What I tell you in the dark, utter in the light; and what you hear whispered, proclaim upon the housetops. And do not fear those who kill the body but cannot kill the soul; rather fear him who can destroy both soul and body in hell.' '' Only in hell can both body and soul be destroyed. In this reality you can kill only the body, the soul will continue to live.

In the book of Ecclesiastes the idea is expressed that life has no purpose other than enjoyment of the pleasures that God has provided on this earth. In Ecclesiastes 12:5-7 a description of the spirit of man is presented in sharp contrast to the physical body.

"Because man goes to his eternal home, and the mourners go about the streets; before the silver cord is snapped, or the golden bowl is broken, or the pitcher is broken at the fountain, or the wheel broken at the cistern, and the dust returns to the earth as it was, and the spirit returns to God who gave it." One portion returns to dust and the other portion returns to God.

In Matthew 27:50, Christ's soul was released from his body. "And Jesus cried again with a loud voice and yielded up his spirit."

Throughout the literature of the major religions, the idea of a clear dichotomy between the spirit and the body is indicated. The two become detached at the moment of death. The religious dichotomy suggests the OOBE found in clinical death, near-death situations, and deathbed observations.

The human soul may leave the body at any sign of hostile actions. The perception of this hostility may be a response to the trauma of clinical death. The cessation of breathing and heartbeats is very disruptive and may cause the soul to be thrust or thrown from the body at the moment death occurs.

Carl G. Jung was a psychologist who attempted to study and report on all sorts of human conditions. He was always interested in the strange qualities of human experience. In 1944 Jung broke his foot and suffered a heart attack. He became very sick as a result of these accidents and subsequently experienced delirium and saw visions. In *Memories, Dreams, Reflections* Jung tells of his experiences while temporarily dead: "My nurse afterwards told me, 'It was as if you were surrounded by a bright glow.' That was a phenomenon she had sometimes observed in the dying she added. I had reached the outermost limit, and do not know whether I was in a dream or an ecstasy. At any rate, extremely strange things began to happen to me."

"It seemed to me that I was high up in space. Far below I saw the globe of the earth, bathed in a gloriously blue light, I saw the deep blue sea and the continents. Far below my feet lay Ceylon, and in the distance ahead of me the subcontinent of India."

Jung later figured that he must have been viewing the earth from 1,000 miles away.

"A short distance away I saw in a space a tremendous dark block of stone like a meteorite. It was about the size of my house or even bigger. It was floating in space, and I, myself, was floating in space. . . . An entrance led into a small antechamber. To the right of the entrance, a black Hindu sat silently in a lotus posture upon a stone bench."

"While I had floated in space, I had been weightless, and there had been nothing tugging at me. And now all that was a thing of the past. I felt resistance to my doctor because he had brought me back to life."

In near-death situations, researchers have reported the detached feelings among a wide range of people in various threatening situations who have thought that their deaths were imminent and certain.

Observations of the spirits of departed loved ones are commonly mentioned by dying patients.

Eileen Garrett writes in her book, *Adventures in the Supernormal*, that she has seen spirals of energy leaving the bodies of the recently-dead. She reports having seen these spirals for up to three days after death.

Billy Graham writes in *Angels:* "At the moment of death the spirit departs from the body and moves through the atmosphere. . . . If the eyes of our understanding were opened, we would probably see the air filled with demons, the enemies of Christ."

Top scientists have attempted to experimentally verify the existence of the soul. Some scientists have been attempting to prove that there are spirits or souls that depart the dying person's body. Other researchers have attempted to capture the elusive soul on its journey out of the body at the moment of death. Ingenious methods used have included photography and sealed rooms and caves. Duncan MacDouball thought that the soul should occupy space and have the physical characteristic of weight. He placed dying patients on a scale to weigh them. As he expected, there was a slow but gradual loss of body weight as the subject died. This is, of course, due to the physiological loss of moisture through breathing and sweating. One patient lost 28 grams of weight per hour. At the moment of death, the subject inexplicably and suddenly lost 21 grams. This experiment was published in the *Journal of the American Society for Physical Research* and reprinted in H. Carrington's *The Coming Science*.

The Kirlian effect was presented to American readers for the first time in Sheila Ostrander and Lynn Schroeder's book, *Psychic Discoveries behind the Iron Curtain*. An electrical aura effect was found around the edges of organic things. The process of photographing this aura is called Kirlian photography. The aura extends around the body and has even outlined a missing finger as though it were still there. Some investigators have hypothesized that this phenomena is the energy of the body or the spirit. The flowing fields of energy gradually fade away after a person's death.

Clairvoyant mediums claim that they can see a person's aura.

Other researchers have found evidence of an electromagnetic field which surrounds all living things.

Other scientists have constructed rooms to study what happens when an animal dies in it. On several occasions the researchers have photographed a wispy cloud over the animal's body which resembled the animal's physical body. There is some evidence of cloud like substances above dying human bodies. These clouds or mists are connected for a while to the physical body, and then, at death they break away.

Most recently, Dr. Charles Tart, of the University of California at Davis, has been conducting experiments in OOBE's. In an article in *Psychic Exploration: A Challenge for Science* (by Edgar Mitchell) Dr. Tart tells how he became convinced that survival after death is possible. He defines OOBE as the ability of one's consciousness to exist outside the physical body and even function away from it.

In his article, "Out-of-the-Body Experiences," Dr. Tart writes: "The effect on a person of having an OOBE is enormous. In almost all cases, his reaction is approximately, 'I no longer believe in survival after death—I know my consciousness will survive death because I have experienced my consciousness existing outside of my physical body.' '' Dr. Tart has become convinced through the study of OOBE's that the soul exists and that it will survive the physical death of the body. This concept is found in many religions.

Dr. Tart describes characteristics of OOBE's: They occur with extreme sicknesses, at near-death, sometimes with meditation. People who have left their bodies tell about floating near the ceiling, looking at their body from the outside, and feeling a normal level of consciousness. Others have often reported seeing loved ones, or beings of light, and the nonexistence of material barriers. They are totally convinced that their experiences were real—that they did not dream it. These characteristics are identical to those experienced by those who have been near-death or clinically dead.

Out-of-body travel was experienced by Sheldon Ruderman of Oakland, California, when he died during cancer surgery. He was embarrassed by his experience with death and OOBE. Now he counsels dying cancer patients on what he saw in the hereafter. His experience is reported in the May 15, 1976 issue of the *National Observer*.

"I'd come into all this a scientist type and an atheist. When you go through an experience like this [death], you think you're crazy. You don't allow these experiences in." Ruderman says he traveled out of his body, watched the doctors operate on him, and wandered about the operating room feeling "free and elated."

Out-of-body experiences give us a clue to the dying process. OOBE's may also let us garner a small glimpse of the Other Side. OOBE's, according to Dr. Russell Noyes (the leading researcher in the area of death-threats to humans), are forms of psychological defense mechanisms for protection of the ego. Noyes argues that when a person is suddenly confronted by the certainty of death, that person alters his perceptions of the physical world to cope with the deadly situation. OOBE's are a method of negating death: We become a spectator to our forthcoming death. Noyes has not completely made up his mind about what his patients are actually experiencing while in these out-of-body travels, but he says, ''The patients' stories are filled with pleasant wonderment.''

In a February 1976 *Psychiatry* article, by Dr. Noyes described his concept of depersonalization in the face of life-threatening situations. In a descriptive analysis of 114 accounts of near-death experiences from 104 people, Dr. Noyes concludes that when death is thought to be a certainty 80% of the people perceived a change in the passage of time; 67% felt a sense of detachment; and 54% felt themselves detach from their bodies and travel away from it.

A stock car driver was involved in a near-tragic accident while traveling at 100 miles an hour. He and the car were thrown into the air and rotated several times before crashing down to the ground. He told Noyes the following story of how it feels to know that you are about to die.

''Everything was in slow motion, and it seemed to me like I was a player on a stage and could see myself tumbling over and over in the car. It was as though I sat in the stands and saw it all happening. I realized I was definitely in danger, but I was not frightened. While I was up in the air, I felt like I was floating . . . into another world.''

The racer was jolted back into this sphere of reality

when his car slammed into the track. The man felt a strong sense of detachment during his flight through the air. At one point, he saw himself upside down. ''I saw the man who won the race pass under me. . . . I can still see the amazed look on his face.'' This feeling of watching events from a distance is similar to those reports made by clinically dead persons who report being able to watch themselves being operated upon.

In Dr. Raymond A. Moody's book, *Life After Life*, a patient recounted his feelings while dead!

''This one morning a solid gray mist gathered around me, and I left my body. I had a floating sensation. . . . I could see myself on the bed below. It was quiet—very peaceful and serene.''

Dr. Elisabeth Kubler-Ross, an internationally known expert on the dying process, believes that she has proof that ''there is life after death.'' In Dr. Kubler-Ross's expert opinion, the existence of the soul or the spirit after death is shown by the fact that patients who were without respiration, brain waves, or heartbeats are able to describe activities and conversations that have occurred around them during the time that they were thought to be completely dead. In a *Newsweek* interview, July 12, 1976, Dr. Kubler-Ross is quoted as saying, ''If you have a woman who has been declared dead in a hospital, and she can tell you exactly how many people walked into the room and worked on her, this cannot be hallucination.''

The president-elect of the American Psychiatric Association, Dr. Robert Gibson, has great respect for Dr. Kubler-Ross's views and opinions concerning clinical death. ''Her research in death and dying is remarkable. It will have enduring value for decades to come.''

According to an interview for the *National Enquirer* on

June 15, 1976, Dr. Kubler-Ross is quoted as saying, "I'm totally convinced that there's life after death. I've seen more than 1,000 people die—and before they died all of them left strong evidence of life after death." One patient who had been totally anesthesized during an operation was able to tell the doctors later about the corrective surgery they had used on her as well as a large portion of the physicians' conversations during the operation.

Dr. Kubler-Ross's explanation for the ability of a patient to describe events that took place while he was unconscious or clinically dead is an out-of-body experience.

Dr. Kubler-Ross also worked with Robert Monroe of Charlottesville, Virginia, in helping terminally ill cancer patients develop out-of-body techniques.

I talked with Mr. Monroe in July of 1976, at the Monroe Institute of Applied Sciences in Afton, Virginia. He told me about his training program.

"I have been working with Dr. Elisabeth Kubler-Ross in helping dying patients to get a glimpse of the hereafter. We have been teaching these patients to leave their physical bodies and explore other realities."

I asked what had been the result.

"Those people who are successful in learning the techniques for leaving their bodies have reported to us that they no longer fear death."

Then I explained: "I have been told that you hold weekend seminars for those wishing to explore out-of-body travel. The people who attend these are not expecting to die in the near future, are they?"

"No, they're just people who would like to experience another reality."

I asked: "What is the difference in your training techniques for those who are dying and those that are presently healthy?''

''We take the terminal cases through a crash program that is just like that we give to the others. We teach the dying to quickly master the ability to leave their painful bodies and experience the bliss found in the spiritual body.''

I wondered if there was a charge for the program.

''Yes, I charge both the regular client and the dying patient. . . . Presently the weekend seminars cost $250.''

Then I asked, ''How much do you charge the dying to leave their bodies?''

This was Monroe's reply: ''My only fee to them is for them to supply me with evidence that they've reached the other realm once they are physically dead in this life.''

Can you imagine the answer I received when I asked: ''Have you received any of those fees yet?''

''Yes. I have gotten proof that those who have died are still existing!''

10
THE BELIEVERS

"I believe in life after death. I have been investigating the phenomena associated with death and the hereafter for most of my life, and I have seen enough evidence to convince even the strongest critic that the soul exists after death," Dr. Karlis Osis of the American Society for Psychical Research told me.

"I also believe that the only way for there to be an existence after death is for the spirit, or if you will, the soul, to depart the body and travel to another reality. Out-of-body experiences and journeys are the only way for this departure of the soul to occur."

I had met Dr. Osis two times before this interview, and I was impressed with the methodology of his research into areas considered outside the realm of "normal" scientific inquiry for "respectable" scientists. But Dr. Osis is very much respected in his profession. His investigations are done under the tightest and best of controlled laboratory conditions. He takes pride in being as scientific and objective as he can, given the unusual nature of the subject. Dr. Osis, a scientist at all times, does believe in continued life after death of the physical container which is the body.

The first time I met Dr. Karlis Osis was at the 1974 convention of the Parapsychological Association held at St. John's University where we were both presenting research briefs concerning our thinking and experiments in the area of psychic phenomena.

Dr. Osis's study was entitled "Perceptual Experiment on Out-of-Body Experiences." He had experimentally tested whether or not out-of-body experiences involve a capability to leave the physical body and make a journey to another point in space. Dr. Osis had used as his subject a Dr. Alexander Tanous, whom a psychic had once reported seeing hovering in a cloud like form over a certain spot.

Dr. Osis used an optical device and a color wheel to test whether Dr. Tanous could see what was being randomly generated in a viewing window. The subject was kept in an isolated and soundproof room at the other end of the building from where the experiment was being held. It was physically impossible to see the object from anywhere except right in front of the viewing window.

During the testing the subject reported the ability to leave his body. He told Osis that ". . . he experienced himself to be without a body, something like being a spot of consciousness, like a light. When this light appears to be very concentrated, like a pin point [Dr. Tanous] felt that he could score well" on the experiment. The subject also reported a feeling of "oneness or unity with existence" while in his out-of-body state.

After the subject mastered the task, his test scores as represented by his ability to read the correct color and optical illusion in the device became significant. It was then concluded that the subject could leave his body, travel to some other physical area, read and understand a message or a concept, and then return to his body with a report of what he had seen.

In the *ASPR* [American Society for Psychical Research] *Newsletter*, Osis writes that there are ". . . subjects whose scoring patterns do support the OOBE hypothesis. However, even among these individuals, none has been able to 'see' the targets the OOBE way every time. It appears that even the most gifted persons achieve true OOBE vision at will only in some tries, not all . . . although subjectively they experience 'being out' on all trials."

OOBE's occur with seriously ill patients, with those on their deathbeds, accident victims, and those who have experienced death and have been resuscitated. Psychiatrists usually label OOBE's as bizarre behavior and place the reports into their files under the category of "Abnormal."

Dr. Karlis Osis has conceptually connected deathbed experiences with OOBE's. He tabulated 877 reports by physicians concerning their patients' last moments. In his analysis, Dr. Osis discovered that patients told about spirits which were coming for their souls. A majority of these patients were not under the influence of drugs, nor were they running any fever. They reported leaving their bodies.

Dr. Osis said, "I see patterns in my research consistent with survival after death."

I contacted Dr. Osis to discuss the possibility of finding proof that the soul existed after death. He told me, "Out-of-b dy experiences are very common reports made by individuals, including those who are not in the process of dying. It is not an easy task to prove to the skeptic that this out-of-body phenomenon does, in fact, exist. I have been investigating OOBE's for many years, and I am convinced that people can actually leave their physical bodies and travel in different levels of reality and consciousness.''

I asked what the physical research on OOBE's had to do with life after death.

''If there is a soul which continues its existence after the person's body dies, then something must actually leave that body. I see a strong relationship or connection between death and OOBE.''

As a first step in discovering that relationship, Osis has investigated the reports of the dying to ascertain what they felt or perceived just before their last moments. Once that was accomplished, he began exploring different experimental methods for proving that OOBE's do exist.

Dr. Osis got his first start with OOBE phenomena when the American Society for Physical Research was awarded a fortune for being able to prove that the soul survives death of the body. The fortune was left by James Kidd, a miner who disappeared several years ago leaving a will which stated that his money was for anyone who could prove the survival of the human soul.

Osis told me that recently he had been studying and experimenting with a very gifted individual living in Baltimore who was able to ''fly-in'' to Osis's New York office and describe target objects that were left on top of the desk. The friend remained physically in Baltimore.

''This man in Baltimore was very successful in telling me what the objects were. He could 'pop' out of his physical body, fly in spirit form to New York, determine the nature of the objects on my desk, and return to Baltimore. He was just recently admitted to a mental hospital in the Baltimore area.

"He lost conscious control over his out-of-body travel. He kept popping out of his body all the time. Once he called collect from the hospital and asked 'Fly with me again.' I got scared after that telephone call, with all that controlled popping out, I quit working with him. I haven't tried any experiments involving 'fly-ins' or OOBE's since that time."

I asked, "How does one learn to leave their body? Is it something that just occurs, or is there a technique for bringing it about?"

"You can learn it. One of the most successful teachers for OOBE is Bob Monroe who has an institute near Charlottesville, Virginia. He holds fairly regular weekend workshops, and he is pretty good at OOBE's. He has traveled out of his body numerous times."

Monroe was originally the subject of experiments conducted by Dr. Charles Tart. As "Mr. X." he wrote *Journeys out of the Body.* In Tart's experiments, Monroe showed evidence of out-of-body travel. During one of the experiments, Monroe reported that one of the lab technicians was out of her room talking to a man, even though she was not to leave that room as long as the experiment was in progress. He could not have known about this unless he had left his body.

I talked with Bob Monroe about his training program and his travels. Monroe believes that he has the ability to leave his body and travel in another realm of energy. He experiences the projection of his soul (or second body).

After working with Dr. Elisabeth Kubler-Ross in the training of terminally ill patients in out-of-body travel, he feels that his OOBE's are the same as those who have died or those who have been almost killed in accidents.

Monroe discussed with me various aspects of his training program. After hearing about Dr. Osis's Baltimore subject, I was especially interested in the inherent dangers in exploring the Other Side.

"I have taught several hundred people how to leave their bodies, and I have never had any problems of that sort. Physical life is infinitely more dangerous than the spiritual life!

"It does alter one's perceptions when he returns to this reality. There is a lasting emotional effect. It is not like a dream at all. It is much more real than a phone conversation."

I wanted to know if there is a way of proving that you have had an out-of-body experience.

"There is no way to prove it happens, nor is there any way to describe the OOBE with words. It must be experienced to be appreciated, but it does happen—my spirit leaves my body, and I travel to another realm."

I asked him, "Have you met others while out-of-body?"

"Yes, I have. But I have never met Jesus or any other religious personages."

Monroe's training program teaches people to enter an energy system which prevails throughout the universe. It is the same kind of energy state that the dying enter upon death.

Monroe has reported his out-of-body ability to exchange sexual energies. In *Journeys out of the Body*, he describes a sexual experience engaged in with a woman while in his "other body." While in his regular bed with his wife, Monroe lifted out of his body and floated into another room where he discovered a willing partner.

"We moved together quickly. There was the giddy electrical-type shock, and then we separated. I thanked her, and she seemed calm and contented. Feeling this was enough for one night, I turned and dived through the floor and soon was reentering the physical [body]."

The next morning Monroe wanted to discover whether he had made love to his houseguest. He asked his wife to go and ask the guest if she was "sexually 'tired.' " It seems that the reason that the guest had come to visit Monroe and his wife was that she was having sex several times every night and she had wanted to get away from the torrid love affair to recuperate and think things over. Monroe did not tell the woman about their sexual-spiritual liaison, but he did notice that she had taken a new interest in him. "Today I caught her staring at me intently again and again, as if she were trying to remember something about me but couldn't."

Dr. Wilhelm Reich was placed in a federal prison (and later died there) trying to publish *The Cancer Biopathy* and other writings discussing his idea that an individual's total health, including that of his mind as well as his body, is possible only with complete sexual satisfaction. Reich felt that sexual orgasm was the focusing element in all the universe. "The elimination of the sexual stasis by the orgastic discharge of the biological excitation removes every kind of neurotic manifestation," Reich writes.

Reich believed that orgone energy flowed throughout the universe and that human sexual relationships merely focused that flow and made for a healthy life. He believed that humans have a need for gratification through "the discharge of excess energy by merging with another organism." Usually this is accomplished by physical sexual intercourse, but more advanced people can have spiritual intercourse which also brings about the merging of energies so necessary for proper health.

In attempting to establish working hypotheses about survival after death, John Palmer in his article "Some Recent Trends in Survival Research," *Parapsychological Review* (May-June, 1975), pointed out the new emphasis in the last few years. Survival research is now related to out-of-body experiences. Experiments have been conducted in which individuals report the sensation of leaving their bodies. Palmer writes: "The OBE (Out-of-Body-Experience is of interest to survival researchers . . . [because] many people who have had OBEs are convinced that they indeed left their bodies." The relationship between survival after bodily death and OBEs is generally accepted by parapsychologists, some psychiatrists such as Elisabeth Kubler-Ross, and even some physicists.

I listened to a couple of physicists explain their OOBE research when I attended the American Parapsychological Association's meeting in Santa Barbara, California in August of 1975. The physicists who gave evidence for the existence of out-of-body travels were Russell Targ and Harold Puthoff.

Every subject that they tested was able to score significantly high on a test where they were required to view a distant object. The research indicated that anyone could leave their physical bodies, journey to some area specified by coordinates, view whatever was there, and return to report on their observations.

Targ and Puthoff are employed at the Stanford Research Institute. Targ is the inventor of some laser equipment and Puthoff invented and patented laser and optical equipment. Their research on "remote viewing" was published by Delacorte Press in a book entitled *Mind-Reach* (1977).

In *Mind-Reach,* the authors described how their participants were able to "picture" target areas in their minds even though they had never before been to these places. They were given nothing more than a set of coordinates in which to determine the location.

The basic phenomenon found by Targ and Puthoff seems to cover the same kind of things that survival researchers are interested in—such as, astral projection, out-of-body experiences, and the experiences of floating and leaving the body reported by those clinically dead.

An interesting discovery was made by the authors of *Mind-Reach*. They wrote that they ". . . never found anyone who could not learn to perceive scenes, including buildings, roads, and people, even those at great distances and blocked from ordinary perception."

In 1930, Upton Sinclair, the author, published his book called *Mental Radio,* in which he described his wife's ability to leave her body and view a distant thing. She had learned a technique (similar to that used by Bob Monroe in his teachings of out-of-body travels) for picking up mental images.

Albert Einstein was so impressed by the Sinclairs' abilities that he wrote the following Preface to *Mental Radio:*

"The results of the telepathic experiments carefully and plainly set forth in this book stand far beyond those which a nature investigator holds to be thinkable. On the other hand, it is out of the question in the case of so conscientious an observer and writer as Upton Sinclair that he is carrying on a conscious deception of the reading world; his good faith and dependability are not to be doubted.'' (May 23, 1930)

The trick, according to Mrs. Sinclair, for leaving one's body was to develop undivided concentration. She saw Jack London's distress even though they were separated by many miles. The same time she saw the distress was the time that Jack London committed suicide.

Mental Radio has been largely ignored for the last forty-seven years because there wasn't a suitable theory to explain Mrs. Sinclair's mental ''seeing'' ability. Now two well respected physicists have designed controlled experiments which accomplish exactly what Mary Craig Sinclair was able to do in 1930. Targ and Puthoff's techniques are similar to those used by Mrs. Sinclair, Reverend Swedenborg, the *Tibetan Book of the Dead*, and the teachings of Bob Monroe in Afton, Virginia.

Mary Craig Sinclair described how she was able to picture distant things and to travel out-of-body. She wrote in *Mental Radio:* ''You have to inhibit the impulse to think things about the objects. . . . The average person . . . has to learn how to do it. Simultaneously, we must learn how to relax, for strangely enough a part of concentration is complete relaxation.''

I decided that I would like to learn how to travel out-of-body. I enrolled in one of Bob Monroe's weekend seminars in December of 1976. It was held in a Holiday Inn in Afton, Virginia.

There are many respected scientists who believe in OOBEs. Dr. Karlis Osis believes that life after death will be in the form of a spirit which can travel without regard for physical constraints and journey out-of-body. In clinical death, near death situations, and at the death bed, the human spirit can spring from the body and speed away into the cosmic universe. But unless we have actually experienced clinical death and felt our departure from the body or experienced an out-of-body event, we must accept the stories of those who have said they have separated from the physical body. It is like accepting a religious doctrine when we attempt to determine what the hereafter is like. We must either experience it ourselves, or we must listen to others and take a leap of faith.

After I had signed up for the Monroe course and arrived at the Holiday Inn, I met the other eleven people who wanted to glimpse the out-of-body world.

I spent the weekend in a bed with a beautiful blond nurse from Chicago on one side of me and a brunette on the other. Both of these women were attempting to learn out-of-body travels.

The others attending the weekend seminar had their own personal reasons for trying to glimpse the Other Side. There was an international banker attending the seminar. I rode back to Charlottesville with the banker and his wife. They were good enough to share their bean sprouts with me.

Also attending the weekend seminar were a hairdresser from Washington, D.C.; a few Ph.D.'s in psychology; and some psychiatrists who have been referred here by Dr. Kubler-Ross.

We all went through the M-5000 program that had us lying on beds Friday, Saturday, and Sunday, listening to tapes with a delta-theta pulsing, and a binaural beat to get both halves of our brains together. Then there was the recorded voice telling me to relax my body and to visualize different patterns. The visualization process was similar to the development of images in the mind.

Targ and Puthoff wrote about the use of imagination in *Mind-Reach* as: "We knew, of course, that there was a phenomenon known as eidetic memory which enabled a person to close his eyes and reproduce complex pictures from memory."

Monroe is building an institute in Afton that will explore the next world. Dr. Elisabeth Kubler-Ross is a member of Monroe's board of directors. They will help the dying to get a preview of the Other Side.

John Palmer wrote a paper entitled "Consciousness Localized in Space Outside the Body," for the *Osteopathic Physician* (April, 1974), in which he said: "Many persons who have had striking OBEs, report that the experience convinced them of survival after death and eliminated their fear of death. Whether or not this conclusion is objectively valid, it does suggest therapeutic possibilities for the OBE. . . . [it] may help persons engaged in high-risk occupations . . . [and] provide comfort to patients in certain stages of terminal illness."

This is just what Kubler-Ross and Monroe have set out to do at the Institute. Monroe has started something called a Star Program. The terminally ill person is rushed through a program similar to what everyone takes but in a more accelerated manner so that the person will quickly gain a perception of what awaits them on the Other Side when they die.

Monroe came in to talk to the group about various topics connected with out-of-body experiences.

"Have fun this weekend," he told the class.

I asked him about the release that we all had to sign not holding the Monroe Institute responsible for any unforeseen difficulties.

"Merely a standard business practice."

The weekend was uneventful for me, unless you call listening to yourself snore something like an out of body experience. Everyone else had great things to say about their experiences. Some flew to see friends several hundred miles away. Others just lifted themselves a short way out of their bodies. I seemed to be the one not being able to get away from himself. I think the rest did me good and I'll probably go back on the mountain some time in the future.

11
THE PERFECT PLACE

"I found myself in the most enchanting place you could ever visit. The beauty was far beyond anything that I had ever seen before in my life. It was so luxuriant that there is absolutely no way to express to you the intense enjoyment I felt with the place. I think that when I die again, I would truly like to return there and spend eternity in that pure and perfect place. I know that I have truly been a visitor to *the* perfect Garden of Eden!"

This sense of the hereafter as perfect was expressed to me by a man named Kenneth G., who had experienced death in a hospital for almost ten minutes. His report on what he saw in the hereafter has been substantiated by his attending physicians and, most importantly, by his daughter Elizabeth, who was of great help to me in putting together this panoramic look at the Other Side.

"I've done a lot of thinking about my visit to that perfect place. I have no recollection of where I might have seen that place before. It seems very strange to me that I could have visited something like that place here on this earth and the memory of it not have been burned forever into my memory.

"I know that my experience was much more than just a dream. I was in the rich, green field surrounded by the aspects of one of my most fond memories. I know that I was transported there by dying. I hope that heaven is like that place—I truly do.

"I discovered myself drifting down to a huge valley. It sloped downward from low, gently rolling hills. There were miles upon miles of the flat rolling plains where I had drifted to, and then I was just standing in this field of soft grass. I was completely alone with my thoughts, but I wasn't lonely. Everything there was pleasant and perfect. It seemed untouched and virginal. It was a natural environment.

"My first conscious thought was that of floating down; down very slowly like a man with a parachute. I drifted out of the sky and landed softly in a field of grass which came up to my waist. It was a delightful sensation. Then I saw that this meadow went on forever.

"I saw dense forests in the far distance. Both the meadow and the forests were filled with all kinds of animals. Bears and beavers, squirrels, cows and horses, dogs, and all other kinds of animals playing together.

"The only word I seem to be able to use to talk about that place is beautiful. It was much more than that word will ever reveal."

I found out about Kenneth G.'s death and experiences while clinically dead through an advertisement I had placed in the *New York Sunday News*.

HAVE YOU HAD 'EXPERIENCES' WHILE NEAR OR CLINI-
CALLY DEAD? WRITER WISHES TO INTERVIEW YOU FOR
BOOK. PLEASE SEND YOUR NAME AND ADDRESS TO:
———————.

I received a letter in response to the notice which I thought was bizarre. It was not in a regular envelope, but instead the writer had taken a ruled sheet of paper, folded it, and placed her message inside of the make-shift envelope. I was hesitant to open the envelope since the writer had sealed it in white surgical tape. I did not want to open a letter which might contain a person's own surgical dressings from their last operation. I had already gotten a letter in response to a *Village Voice* advertisement from a person who supposedly had a roommate who was starving himself to death because he was being controlled by the Korean CIA. "He is not violent, what should I do?" that letter had read. But I did open Elizabeth C.'s letter. And I am glad that I opened it and read what she had to say.

"I am a nurse, and my father was expired for ten minutes in _____ Hospital. He was successfully resuscitated, and he gave those around him a very clear explanation of what he saw while he was dead. . . . This incident is documented and recorded by one of New York's most respected physicians. I think that my father would talk to you if you don't harass him or annoy him. Death has always mystified me, and I could not resist writing you. Please excuse this letter's form as I had no envelopes, and I wanted to respond as soon as possible." The letter included Elizabeth's telephone number and address.

I called Elizabeth the next day and told her about my research on people who had died and promised not to bother her father. She told me what she knew of her father's experiences while dead.

"Daddy had gone to the racetrack that day. On the way home, he had a heart attack. They found him lying on a street and called for an ambulance. On the way to the hospital he lapsed into a coma. Upon arrival at the hospital, they placed him in the Intensive Care Unit while they ran tests on him to determine the nature of his sickness. A couple of hours later he came out of the coma on his own, and the doctors decided that he would be all right in one of the regular hospital rooms. There was nothing they could do that night since it appeared that he was doing okay. During the night, he died.''

I wanted to know how long he had been dead.

''Maybe as long as ten minutes, but for at least seven according to the nurses.''

I was a little skeptical about this. The human brain suffers damage within four or five minutes after the heart stops delivering oxygen to it. In an earlier case, I've mentioned Victor Solow who was dead for twenty-three minutes. But he was manually pumped on the chest to keep the blood circulating, carrying oxygen.

Elizabeth explained.

''The attending physicians thought that he was most likely dead for four or five minutes. We don't know how he came out of this without brain damage, but he did. In fact, he thinks a little clearer than before he died.

''We know that he was checked by one of the nurses at 10:30, and he was definitely still alive. Ten minutes later we found him slumped out of the bed and dead.''

One of his doctors said, ''The patient's body was black in spots indicating that the blood had ceased flowing through the body. The blood had already started to settle in the body's lower portions. If I did not know Elizabeth personally, I do not think that we would have attempted to resuscitate the man. He was as dead as anyone that I have ever seen. I saw no real hope but decided to go ahead as though there was. I don't think that Elizabeth would have forgiven me if I hadn't tried to bring her dad back to life. I was amazed when he snapped out of his death so quickly."

When he did revive, Kenneth related a powerful story of the hereafter to those gathered around his hospital bed. He told of a place where a glorious nature had been blended with memories of his past experiences.

Kenneth told those around him: "When I go again, please leave me alone and let me stay in that next world!"

He went into an elaborately detailed account of the things that he saw that induced him to want to die again. He told the doctors: "I floated down to a grassy field which had horses, cows, lions, and all kinds of wild and tame animals. It was a painting at first, then it became real. I was in that field looking at all those great things when you pulled me back. Around the border of the valley I could perceive the intrusions of the experiences of my past. I saw things that had not been thought about for 50 to 60 years."

The doctors recorded the entire conversation and filed it away. They were, of course, thankful that Kenneth G. had returned to the land of the living and attributed his tales and reports on his experiences to hallucinations caused by oxygen starvation.

It is true, of course, that images and strange thoughts are created in a person's mind who is deprived of oxygen for a short while. Pilots and deepsea divers experience rapture of the deep when they have their air cut off. They see visions that don't exist for those with plenty of air.

Hallucinations are false sensory inputs. The person sees things that don't exist. In schizophrenia, a patient may hear comments on his behavior. He'll hear obscene names, orders given, or messages from secret organizations may be received. For decades it has been assumed that people who hallucinate are crazy. But with the recent sophistication in the behavioral sciences, partly due to parapsychology, we are gradually changing our ideas of the universe. We now know that the pseudo-inputs of the schizophrenic merely reflect the unconscious fear of the individual patient.

Psychiatrists usually utilize Freud's notion of defense mechanisms to explain patients' behavior in seeing green, lush fields when that patient has never left the confines of the hospital. Or they may say it is due to an active imagination, dreaming, and the like.

But, based on the insights of Elisabeth Kubler-Ross, people who see things while clinically dead are now thought to be having a look at the Other Side, and not simply conjuring those views up in their own minds.

Elizabeth G. gave me some background information on her father during my first conversation with her. He had lived most of his life in Sheepshead Bay, part of Brooklyn. Since the nineteenth century, it has been a popular fishing and recreation area with new fields. Elizabeth said, "He described to us flowers that I'm sure that he had never seen in his life. He was never very interested in horticulture or things like that. I am very surprised that he was even aware of nature. It is not something that an unconscious mind would cause fantasies about. He was always interested in machinery, not aesthetic things."

There were other things that Kenneth G. told the physicians and his family that struck Elizabeth as being too coincidental to be tossed off lightly. Elizabeth continued,

"When he came out of the death state, he told us that he had heard some very faint noises. He finally recognized the noises as the voice of his father. The voice kept faintly telling him, 'Kenneth, don't be afraid. I have come to help you with your journey. Don't be afraid of this. I've helped others.' "

"I thought that was pretty strange. Father never knew this, but when grandfather was dying, the same thing happened. Just before passing away, he told the minister that he faintly heard someone calling to him. He didn't tell us who the voice belonged to. My grandfather had been dead ten years when father heard him faintly calling to him from that other place."

Another thing which had intrigued Elizabeth was the mention of a stream of water that her father had been walking toward just as he was brought back to life. Kenneth said, "I was coming toward a stream in this field. I thought to myself, 'My feet are about to get wet.' "

Elizabeth said, "When my uncle was dying, he was lucid up to the final moment. He had a glazed and distant look in his eyes, but he seemed rational and coherent about what was happening to him. He told the nurse, 'My feet are getting wet. Help me, I'm drowning.' Before the nurse could walk the three feet to his bed, he was dead.

"My father saw the next world. I know it, and I believe it. And it's too much a coincidence for these members of my family to talk about water in connection with death."

I received a call from Kenneth G. the day after my conversation with his daughter. I let him describe the next world as he had seen it, as fully as he could.

"As I stood there in the middle of this lush, green field, I could see animals, flowers, and trees. It was the flowers that I especially liked. I'd never before seen anything like the profusion of growing beautiful plants and flowers in this place.

"For a while I stood in that waist-high grass, listening to the gentle rustle of grass being blown by a light breeze. That, for a while, was the only sound. Then I heard a voice calling to me. It was at first so faint that I just felt that someone was trying to talk to me. It got a little louder. I did not see the person calling to me, but I recognized the owner of the voice. It was my father who had died ten years ago. 'What is he doing here?' I thought to myself. Here am I in a strange meadow. I don't know where I am, and my dead father is calling to me. I accepted things as they were—what else could I do?

"The voice told me, 'Do not worry, I have come to help you.'

"The meadow appeared just like it had been washed by a cleansing morning rain. Clean. Spotless. Perfect. There was nothing to mar its attractiveness. It felt good to be there even though I was all alone.

"Then, some joyous laughter rolled across the meadow and caught my attention. I looked across the grass and up the slight curvature of the hill in the distance. There, in a broad expanse which was separated from the trees, I saw children playing in an amusement park. They looked very familiar.

"I saw little boats with small white sails. The boats were only just large enough to hold two people. They were sailing back and forth on a small lake which separated the natural-appearing elements of the field, meadow, and forest from that park in the distance. The park was like one that I remembered as a child. You know what Steeplechase Park in Coney Island once looked like? I heard kaleidoscope music coming across the field, carried by the wind. There were no cars in this park. But all my old playmates were there, just like they were sixty years ago. But I recognized them as being old. They appeared young as they played, but their physical appearance was like my most recent memory of them. It was old and young merged together. None of them noticed me; they continued to play in the amusement park as we had done half a century ago. It reminded me of those parks like Disneyland. I remembered my years as a boy fifty years ago in Coney Island, and I remembered Lunar Park of fifty years ago—the 'Fun Place for the Nation.' I stood in a field and saw clowns in a mystical park—a fairyland place where there were goodies available that we used to like as kids.''

I asked Kenneth, ''Were you happy being in this strange world?''

''I was filled with happiness, and I was really there.''

I wondered about the smell of the meadow and flowers.

''I could smell the forests and the grasses and the flowers. Everything smelled fresh. It was very pleasant and not overpowering. There were flowers of all colors everywhere, but I had trouble smelling anything but the fresh grass that I was standing in. The field was covered in a carpet of flowers, the likes of which I have never seen. Also, there were huge oak trees. Trees like we kids used to build our swings and tree houses in. They were as big as a house. Trees big enough to play under and on.''

Then I asked, ''Did you notice any fears or discomforts associated with being a stranger in a strange place?''

''No, I knew I was supposed to be there. I just knew that this was my place, and I belonged there.''

I asked Kenneth to describe anything else he saw.

"Around the edges of the forests that surrounded the meadow that I was standing in I could see buildings, tall buildings like those of Manhattan's skyline in the Battery Area. I saw those little boats in the channel."

Since Kenneth grew up in Brooklyn, it was natural that he should remember seeing Manhattan from where he played.

"I was a little boy again, reliving the youth that I found most pleasant. That was most interesting since I carried with me all those experiences a lifetime of living to sixty-two years old brings with you. There was an odd blend of the new and the different mixed with my fond old memories—thoughts that were the best things of my life. I have a theory that nothing is really as good as we remember them to be in our dreams.

"The sky was pure blue. Not the blue you see in the polluted skies today, but a real blue—sharp, clean, and pure in color. Sharply outlined in the skies were the pure white clouds gracefully moving across the skies. It was a perfect place in which to spend an eternity.

"The flowers were everywhere, and they were so natural looking and perfect, one could actually pick them. I swear, it had to be heaven. I was in a field of my desires—standing among the greenest, lushest, most vibrant colors. The time was late May or early June. I was there before the hot, dry summer had a chance to bleach everything out to look yellow and dead."

I asked Kenneth if he would like to go back.

"Yes, of course. When I woke, the only thing that I could think about was how wrong it was for them to bring me back from such a wonderful, contented place. The kids who were playing in my memories were howling with joy. My soul was filled with love and happiness.

"There were blue flowers, goldenrods with their heads yellow in color, and the flowers arranged in perfect pyramid clusters. Elsewhere in that most perfect of places, I saw Queen Anne's lace being circled by large, graceful butterflies. I can't remember being in such a beautiful area of nature. There was thick, green moss luxuriously growing on the sides of the rocks on the hills and on the trees. There were wild violets, bluebirds, robins, and sparrows. Everything that was good and natural I saw in the meadow and the surrounding forests.

"There I was, standing in the midst of morning watching the pale dewdrops clinging to the grass which glistened like precious jewels reflecting the light in different ways.

"I was approaching a small stream which was as smooth as a mirror lying flat and reflecting a perfect setting from its surface. Just behind the stream were the hickories, oaks, and tall, silent trees of the forest. The forest was bright and not foreboding at all. Nothing about this place was dark; nothing was frightening. I have been to florists and seen flower arrangements. The flowers in my paradise were natural but as perfect as those in the florists' baskets.

"Once again I heard the kaleidoscopic music being carried across the expanse of the field. My attention went to the happy children once again. They played like I played when I was younger. Now, they were more like spirits. They were really there in the amusement park with clowns and the huge friendly elephant, just the same as fifty years ago. I felt happiness with that memory. I saw

Lunar Park amusements. I could see Jumbo the Elephant at the back of the park, just like he was there half a century ago. God, it was beautiful!

"Death seemed to have blended the hereafter with the fondest memories I carried through life. I know I went to heaven with my most cherished childhood memories.

"A red dragonfly darted out of the distance and came toward me with increasing speed. It came straight toward my face. It got larger and larger until, smashing into my face, I was brought back to this world and this life."

Upon being resuscitated, Kenneth G. could not understand why the doctors were there. It took some explaining to convince Kenneth that he had died on his hospital bed and they had to shock him back to life. For a long time he wouldn't accept the fact that he had never left his bed.

It hardly seems decent to have done this to Kenneth. To bring him back from the perfect place, the Other Side, and make him live the way he has to do now. He is confined to a wheelchair as a result of a greatly weakened heart. For nine months after the death, he was told to stay in a wheelchair and not to take a step nor to move himself. He is too weak to take care of himself.

The experience with death has changed him somewhat. He is no way bitter about being brought back to life; he knows what is there, and he will wait for the next chance to visit the Other Side and walk in the fields of happiness.

But Kenneth now says, "I once took everything very seriously. Before dying, I did not want to cause anyone any problems, and I sometimes went too far out of my way for the convenience of others. I realized that I had wasted some of the more important years of my life. During the second World War, I wasted five years in the United

States Army. I was in the transportation corps. I took live and well soldiers to Europe, and I brought back the dead and the seriously wounded.

"I don't take things as seriously now. I let them call me. I was in the hospital for six months, and I incurred a tremendous bill. It does not worry me to know that I am deeply in debt. My paradise is waiting!

"When I was there, I felt like part of that world. I watched things occur, but I was only there to watch. I knew my place. The only indication I received that someone else was aware of my presence was my father's voice which reassured me that he was there to help in my journey. I approached that stream of water just as a passenger on a train might approach the bridge over a river. I was completely and totally conscious of the event, but I had nothing which would allow me to alter its inevitable outcome."

I wanted to know about his physical appearance in the hereafter.

"I don't really know. There were no mirrors available. I know that I was standing upon the ground, and therefore, I must have something like feet, but the waist-high grass obstructed my vision.

"I was walking toward the stream, and I knew that there was something more waiting for me on the other side of the stream."

"Something more? Like what?" I wondered.

"I don't know, I just know that my experience in the hereafter was incomplete. A feeling came over me that complete understanding of the universe was just on the other side of that water. Once I got my feet wet and crossed that stream, my journey would be complete."

Kenneth G.'s account of the Other Side is a curious blend of something completely new to him and something old. There was the meadow and valley in which he found himself, filled with flowers of many kinds that he had never seen before and all sorts of animals. He knew that he was not dreaming the vivid account of this paradise. The old was the almost forgotten memory of the past when he was a young boy playing with his friends in Brooklyn, New York.

It could be said that the effects of physiological death caused a trauma in the neurological system of the body which resulted in hallucinations mixed with memories so that Kenneth G. perceived himself as being in a place that was new to him while at the same time filled with memories of his past.

Indeed, there is experimental evidence showing the effects of stimulation in producing in vivid detail a panoramic vision and memories of past events that may have seemed completely forgotten.

In 1946 the Canadian neurologist Penfield was able to bring forth complex memories in the patients he was operating on. He did this by electrically stimulating points in the cortical tissue of the temporal lobe of the brain. One of his patients reported hearing in great detail a concert that he had attended thirty years before. When he electrically excited the brain of another of his patients, Penfield reported the man as saying: "Dream is starting—there are a lot of people in the living room—one of them is My Mother."

But conjectures of this sort are wasted on people like Elizabeth G. She knows that her father was dead for several minutes. She knows that his soul left his body and traveled to the place where the rolling fields of the hereafter blended with her dad's memories of his past. She knows that he had visited his heaven for a while. And she knows that he will return there sometime in the future.

12
SEARCHES FOR
THE OTHER SIDE

The Spaniards landed near Vera Cruz in 1519, and they destroyed the Aztec civilization mercilessly. Montezuma II, who was the last Aztec emperor, was killed in 1520. The Aztecs believed that the fate of their dead in the hereafter depended on how they died. Prisoners captured for sacrifice as well as women dying in childbirth automatically entered paradise. Once there, they spent eternity as pretty hummingbirds and butterflies. Others entered the land of the dead, but theirs was not an easy journey.

For the Aztecs, the Journey to the Other Side was sometimes a difficult one. Papers were placed on the corpse to help him in his journey. With the aid of the papers, the person could pass the two mountains which clashed together, by a serpent in a road, through a lair of the green lizard, over eight deserts and eight hills, as well as through the place where winds were driven with obsidian knives. This was the journey for the average Aztec to the underworld. When the souls arrived before the god Mictlantecuhtli, they were helped by the god's dog to enter the house of the dead.

The Aztecs are remembered for their human sacrifices, which they thought were necessary to keep the sun in its place. To the victims, sacrifice meant a glorious hereafter—a sure ticket to the Other Side. Even prisoners captured by the Aztecs considered it an honor to be sacrificed to the gods.

After 1520, the Spaniards put a halt to the sacrifices and attempted to convert the Aztecs to ideas of European culture.

The Indians told the Spaniards many tales of rich cities and strange places to the north where great amounts of gold and silver could be found. Whether there really were such places or whether the Indians lied to keep the Spaniards searching, we don't know.

The Spanish searched throughout the Americas looking for gold. Any story concerning that magical substance immediately got their undivided attention. The Islands of the Seven Cities, sometimes called Antillia—Land of Gold, were shown in an early map drawn by Johannes Martines of Messian around 1578. This is the map of the Seven Cities of Cibola, or the Seven Cities of Gold, which lured the Spaniards to search for golden cities.

Many of the tribes of the Americas are rich in mythological tales of how they began from these Seven Cities. The Indians of Mexico believe that their ancestors dwelt there.

The Indians of the New World were filled with stories that kindled the imaginations of the Spanish explorers. There was a story about the magical waters of the Fountain of Youth for which Juan Ponce de Leon searched through the swamps and wilds of Florida.

Many of the Indians' stories are similar to stories in the Bible about the hereafter. The legend of the Golden Cities is similar to the Book of Revelation's description of heaven.

The legend of the Golden Cities of Seven is described by Pedro de Castaneda in *Spanish Explorers in the Southern United States*. In 1530, the president of New Spain owned Tejo, an Indian from the valley of Oxitipar. "This Indian said he was the son of a trader who was dead, but that when he was a little boy, his father had gone into the back country with fine feathers to trade for ornaments and that when he came back, he brought a large amount of gold and silver of which there is a good deal in that country. He went with him once or twice and saw some very large villages which he compared to Mexico and its environs. He had seen seven very large towns which had streets of silver-workers."

Stephen Clissold's *The Seven Cities of Cibola* describes an encounter with an alleged citizen of the strange city. It was described as a "great city where the entrances and fronts of the buildings are made of turquoise." The Spaniards searched and found only the adobe walls of the Pueblo Indians.

In *Coronado's Children*, the famous south-western writer J. Frank Dobie, writes about the travels of the Spanish explorer Cabeza de Vaca. "Somewhere to the north [of Mexico] was a galaxy of cities, the inhabitants of which wore civilized raiment, lived in places ornamented with sapphires and turquoise, and possessed gold without end—the Seven Cities of Cibola." Cabeza de Vaca told of the wonders of these cities that were sometimes many stories tall. The gold was so plentiful that the natives tipped their arrows with it.

Francisco Vasquez de Coronado traveled throughout the deserts and plains of the Southwest in 1540, seeking the fabled Seven Cities of Cibola. While in New Mexico he heard the story of a city called "Quivira" where there was more gold than in all of Peru. An Indian guide named Turk led Coronado and his men through the wilds of North America. When they found only savages living in mud huts, they removed the Turk's head. The authorities were so upset over Coronado's failure to find any cities of gold that they charged him with gambling and playing dice while on his travels. He also was charged with failure to collect taxes from the natives that he met on his way.

The Indians have a legend about a force which keeps all but a selected few from being able to see the golden cities. Indian witchcraft and the "Spirit of the Dead" make the cities invisible unless one experiences the proper spiritual transformation. Chewing on peyote is said to alter one's vision enough to be able to see the Other Side. Spirits of the dead are able to see the Seven Cities of Cibola and the Grain Quivira in their golden splendor. Dying Indians have reported these as visions.

The gold which was the object of the search for the legendary cities may be considered nothing more than the work of a fertile Indian imagination. There was no gold discovered covering the streets and houses of the Indian villages.

But maybe there is a magic which keeps away the nonbeliever.

Stephen Clissold writes: "They say that the witchcraft

of the Indians is such that when they come by these towns they cast a mist upon them so that they cannot see them.''

Maybe the Indian tales were true. In his report to the Senate Select Committee on Presidential Activities (on the Watergate fiasco) John Dean said the exploration party headed by F. Lee Bailey had discovered a hoard of gold hidden in the New Mexico desert. They had estimated that one hundred tons of it lay buried on a military installation not far from the Trinity Site and just a few miles from the Gran Quivira, one of the golden cities.

Legends always contain some truth. The Indians' view of the cities on the Other Side may be more than just a good religious story—it may represent visits by those peyote-chewing Indians to the actual place.

Throughout the world there are groups who believe that the doorway to understanding the next world (the hereafter or the ''separate reality'') can be found through the proper use of magical drugs in religious ceremonies. Drugs enhance the mystical feelings of religion and they become another pathway to glimpsing at the Other Side. Other methods of discovering the hereafter are found, of course, in death, near-death situations, meditation, out-of-body experiences, and dreaming.

If the human spirit merely resides in a physical body temporarily, as some theologians and philosophers have suggested, then that spirit may move out of that body when the time is ripe or the death of the body is imminent. Altering one's state of awareness or consciousness with drugs, meditation, or prayer has been suggested as a way of entering the spiritual world—the world of the dead.

Hallucinogenic and psychedelic drugs are mind-altering substances. Mescaline, a hallucinogenic substance, is derived from the peyote cactus (Lophophora Williamsii) and it produces profound changes in the perception of the user. People who have chewed on the buds of the peyote report religious experiences. "I see a spirit descending from the sky. The world is filled with happiness."

In pre-Columbian times, the Aztec Indians ate the peyote ceremonially and behavioral and psychic changes resulted. During these drug-induced states, doorways were opened to the Other Side. Then the Aztec Indians could see gem-covered walls and streets of silver which they told the Spaniards about.

In 1954, Aldous Huxley described his use of the peyote cactus to alter his way of seeing the world in *The Doors of Perception*. Huxley's mystical views about peyote (mescaline) included his belief in its power to open doors to other worlds. Huxley writes: "The other world to which mescaline admitted me was not the world of visions; it existed out there, in what I could see with my eyes open. The great change was in the realm of objective fact. What had happened to my subjective universe was relatively unimportant."

In ancient Mexico mescaline from the peyote cactus was used for hundreds of years for divination, communications with the powers in the next world, and religious improvement.

The Aztecs used specialists who saw the Other Side through visions brought about by the powerful peyote cactus. For years after the Spanish conquest of Mexico, communal ceremonies using peyote continued.

The Mescalero Apache started using peyote in their ceremonies about 1870. A member of the Yaqui tribe encountered a ''power''—a giver of visions—who taught the Indian the uses of the mystical plant.

In the 1870's, enterprising importers were supplying magical peyote to interested buyers for a nickel a bud. Later, the eager young of the drug-oriented culture of the 1960's discovered the hallucinatory effects of the cactus and started taking their own trips to heaven.

A few years ago, one could go to the local garden supply in Texas and purchase a cactus that would help you visit the Other Side, just as it had helped the Indians for centuries.

When the government discovered the kind of enjoyment some people were getting from the little cactus buds, it quickly stepped in to stop the sales. It became illegal to purchase those little plants and illegal to eat them. For a while even the Indians were stopped from the legal use of their sacred cactus. This was as bad to the Indians as the government stopping the Catholics from using wine at their masses.

After legal discussions, it was finally decided that a recognized member of the Native American Church could continue using peyote buds in religious ceremonies. Otherwise, you could not use that plant for instant nirvana.

Now, in religious ceremonies of the Native American Church, a button from the peyote cactus is placed in an alter and through the night the Indians sing, pray, and then slowly chew on the plant to ''get nearer to the next world and God.''

Carlos Castaneda made an extensive study of the Indians' use of the mystical peyote cactus. He described his experiences with peyote in *The Teachings of Don Juan: A*

Yaqui Way of Knowledge. Castaneda tells how he was able to alter his method of perception and see the Other World.

"Whatever is contained in the cactus Lophophora Williamsii had nothing to do with me in order to exist as an entity; it existed by itself out there, at large. I knew it then. At one point I was almost vaporous, I was being pushed up toward a light . . . until finally it erupted into what I recognized as the sun coming out from behind the mountains."

Indians see everything in their world as having religious significance. Each object in the universe is animated by some spirit which can be contacted through their prayers, and the peyote helps in contacting those spirits.

Understanding of the hereafter can be gained through study of traditional Indian religion, especially through the numerous legends and rituals. The Navajos have a thousand legends that tell of spiritual afterlife and of the creation of the world and the universe.

A peyote rite spread through central Mexico up to the Rio Grande. Today, Indians worship God who put some of His power in peyote.

After eating the sacred peyote, the Indians see visions similar to those seen by the clinically dead, those experiencing near-death, and those traveling out-of-body. They overestimate time. Ideas of various kinds rapidly enter their brains. In *The Peyote Cult*, Weston LaBarre says that the religious experience which accompanies peyote-eating leads to "an indescribable feeling of dual existence." He continues: "thus after sitting with closed eyes subjectively examining the color visions, on suddenly opening them for a brief space one seems to be a different self, as on waking from a dream we pass into a different world from that in which we have been.'' Users of the sacred peyote have a feeling of detachment and of a heightened perception of the world.

According to legends, God gave the Indian peyote for the purpose of strengthening the Indian's religion. It was a sacred thing first brought to the Indians by a woman. Women always have a place in peyote worship.

Adamson Hoebel was allowed to partake of the peyote along with some of the Cheyenne tribesmen of Montana. It is a form of communion with the Great Spirit who gave the Indian peyote. In his article ''The Wonderful Herb: An Indian Cult Vision Experience,'' Hoebel described the mystical visions and feelings that came to him when he ate four peyote plants and opened the doorway to the Other Side. ''The veil beyond which the white man may not see had been parted for me . . . the peyote had come to me.''

Hobel entered the sacred place with the Indians. They ate the peyote and the world changed.

''Who had entered the lodge in mortal clothing were now perceivable as graven images. I sat among gods in the conclaves of another time. Suddenly all was clear to me. The fire was no longer its ordinary red and yellow. Flames danced in royal purple and emerald green, proud in their beauty. Even the tinder took on a transcendental notion. The butt of a burning stick transfigured to the open-mouthed head of a timber wolf grinned at me through the kaleidoscopic flames.''

Hoebel became fascinated with the powers of peyote. It took him away from the white man's world and its veiled coverings. It opened up to him the spirit world of the Indian.

"The ground before me began a slow revolution. The quilt upon which I sat was no longer a soiled rag, for I was being lifted on a magic carpet. The stars above cavorted in choreographic patterns against the cobaltic sky. . . . The straw on the ground moved towards me in strands of gold. Then with a blinding flash it flowed in a wild vortex from which fused such an exquisite leaf pattern as no worker in the precious metal has ever wrought!''

Hoebel became convinced that there was something good in peyote, something which God had placed in the plant and that He had instructed the Indians to use for strengthening their religions. Part of the instruction was that peyote must not be eaten just to get a good feeling.

Weston LaBarre believes that peyote is less harmful than tobacco and alcohol. "And as for his mental health, western man is already embedded in narcotic institutions such as advertising, television, and movies—which invite illusions about ourselves fully as dangerous as any Indian religious cult.''

The Soux Indian's mythology includes a Ghost Dance Religion. A portion of this Ghost Dance includes the doctrine given by the messiah himself to the believers. "Do not tell the white people about this. Jesus is now upon the earth. He appears like a cloud. The dead are alive all again. I do not know when they will be here . . . . Do not refuse to work for the whites and do not make any trouble with them until you leave them. When the earth shakes [with the coming of the new world] do not be afraid. It will not hurt you. Do not tell lies.'' (From the 1896 report of James Mooney, "The Ghost-Dance Religion and the Soux Outbreak of 1890,'' written for the Bureau of American Ethnology in Washington, D.C., 1896).

Those who have died for a brief moment and then have been resuscitated tell about the detachment of their spirits. A separation of body and soul similar to that felt by those who have touched death for a moment is clearly part of the Indian religious experience. The Indians' beliefs concerning their souls may have sprung from one of their own brothers, who may have died for an instant in battle or accident and somehow come back to life to tell about his journey to the Other Side.

The Indians never doubted the separate immoral existence of their spirits or souls, but they did not propose the probable state or condition of the hereafter. The white man invented the concept of the Indians' "happy hunting ground." Charles Eastman, whose Indian name was Ohiyesa, explored the Indians' concept of the hereafter in a short book entitled *The Soul of the Indian*. "The primitive Indian was content to believe that the spirit which the 'Great Mystery' breathed into man returns to Him who gave it, and that after it is freed from the body, it is everywhere and prevades all nature, yet often lingers near the grave of "spirit bundle" for the consolation of friends, and is able to hear prayers. So much of reverence was due the disembodied spirit, that it is not customary with us even to name the dead aloud."

According to Eastman, many of the Indians believed in reincarnation. Some, through trances and peyote ceremonies, were able to have full knowledge of a former life. According to Charles "Ohiyesa" Eastman, his Indian brothers were able to talk with their "twin spirits" from other races or tribes.

One Soux prophet of war told of having a spirit brother among the Ojibways, who were the enemies of the Sioux.

During one of their hunts, he forewarned his tribe of meeting with the enemy tribe led by his twin spirit. The two tribes did meet. The two prophets met one another. The stranger began singing the very same song as did the Sioux prophet. "This proved to the warriors beyond doubt or cavil the claims of their seer."

Most present-day researchers are very skeptical of reincarnation reports, especially those given by an individual who, under hypnosis, tells about an earlier life in another body.

Dr. Alexander Matos, past president of the American Hypnotist Association and former publisher of *Scientific Hypnosis Magazine*, discounts all stories of previous existence.

"The human mind is very susceptible to the power of the hypnotist's commands. The hypnotized individual tries very hard to please the hypnotist, even to the extent of developing stories out of the forgotten recesses of the unconscious mind. I don't believe that we can ever prove those reports of reincarnation."

In more than one instance, people who regress backwards in their lives have had traumatic things happen. In one experiment, researchers wanted to learn more about one man's memory of a time when he died of a heart attack. The researchers used hypnosis to take the individual back to that time when he was stricken and clinically dead for about five minutes. During the regression hypnosis, the man was again striken by a heart attack, just as he had been two years before!

We cannot separate myth from historical fact. The Indians' stories of their journeys to the hereafter may have certain elements of truth in them. But they are no more or less believable than those of other religious doctrines. Maybe there are separate doorways to the land of the dead, and death and the peyote vision are but two of the ways to get there from here.

The account of the hereafter related by Richard Pratt, an Arapaho Indian, was recorded by Alice Marriott and Carol K. Rachlin in their book, *American Indian Mythology*.

"When people die, they must go over a hill. There is a dividing line between the world we live in and the world of those who have gone before us. That line is the crest of a hill. In the old days . . . there was just the line of rocks on the crest of the hill. Nowadays, when all the country is fenced, there is a line of barbed wire there to mark the boundary. When someone is very sick, he may start climbing the hill. If he reaches the top of the hill, he can look across to the other side. The downhill slope is easy, and the grass grows thickly all the way to the bottom. At the bottom is a river."

Mr. Pratt described how the sick man would be implored by friends and relatives of his who had died to join them in the village just across that stream. "The living can hold him if they beg hard enough." Pratt said that the necessity to decide between returning to life and joining those in the Indian village beyond the stream arose for him twice. Once in Saipan during the Second World War and again in Korea.

Most Indian religions do not present a view consistent with that of the Protestant religion, namely, that of heaven and a hell.

"There is no difference in the afterlife of the good and the bad; all share the same world after death. It is the Arapaho way not to judge people."

Religion has been an important aspect of life of the American Indian. It affects all aspects of their lives. Indians believe in the spirits and gods which they reach through the proper rites and prayers.

The Hopi who wants to join the spirits of his loved ones in the beyond must keep his heart pure and be good to others. When the Hopi dies, as the last breath leaves the body, if he has been bad, two witches take him to their country which is a bad place. He thirsts eternally. No one waters him.

The Plains Indians were nomadic hunting tribes who went on vision quests where they would spend a week fasting alone in hopes of glimpsing spirits from the Other Side.

The Sun Dance of the Plains Indians was a petition to the spirits to improve man's lot on earth.

The Winnebago Indians believed that the dead person's spirit is carefully told about the road ahead to the other world just after his death. According to legend, the journey starts in the morning. The spirits explain: "As you proceed from the place [where the person died], the spirits will come to meet you and take you to the village where the chief lives. There you will give him the tobacco and ask for those objects of which we spoke to you. There you will meet all the relatives who have died before you. They will be living in a large lodge. This you must enter." This is from Paul Radin's *The Winnebago Tribe*.

We see in this legend similarities with the reports of the resuscitated dead and those experiencing deathbed visions. When someone dies, a spirit of a departed loved one comes to aid the traveler in arriving at the Other Side.

The visions of Indians who use peyote and fast on

mountains are not too far removed from contemporary reports of people experiencing out-of-body travel. Indian mythology and legends may be as close to the truth about the hereafter as reports of the Other Side learned from the other out-of-body travelers.

13
THE RELIGIOUS EXPERIENCE

"When I felt myself die, part of something within pulled out from my body and moved up and away from the bed. I became a little like a cloud, very wispy, with not too much in the way of distinct form. I moved up and up at increasing speed. I traveled for a long time through what I think was this tunnel. After a while I stopped moving and just floated there. I felt other beings around me. I felt the presence of the King of the Universe. I felt the power move through me. I knew I was in the presence of pure energy. I was truly moved by the experience. I saw only a bright—ever so bright—light just before I found myself in my body on a bed again. I was surrounded by people."

This mystical experience is just one case where an individual who died felt the presence of some more powerful spirit. God has spoken to some of the clinically dead. He has guided others in their journeys to the Other Side.

Proof of the existence of the Other Side is found in the religious experiences of other people. In fact, according to

Owen S. Radcliff, professor at New York University, "We are not interested in individuals' religious experiences unless *proof* of the hereafter is offered."

We don't have to actually experience death to see and know the next world. Moses, Cotton Mather, Joseph Smith, Jr., and Billy Graham are some of the better known individuals who have been shown or told about the hereafter. Our acceptance of their stories depends on our belief in the same religious concepts. It's a matter of faith.

In the Bible, we see that Moses was contacted by the Lord's emissary and then by God:

"And the angel of the Lord appeared to him in a flame of fire out of the midst of a bush; and he looked, and lo, the bush was burning, yet it was not consumed. And Moses said, 'I will turn aside and see this great sight, why the bush is not burnt.' When the Lord saw that he turned aside to see, God called to him out of the bush, 'Moses, Moses!' And he said, 'Here am I.' Then he said, 'Do not come near; put off your shoes from your feet, for the place on which you are standing is holy ground.'" (Exodus 3:2-5)

Moses was personally told by God of the existence of a hereafter. Then, once Moses had delivered the people of Israel out of Egypt, Moses went up on Mount Sinai to receive the Ten Commandments from God.

The Reverend Cotton Mather was a Puritan preacher who lived from 1663 to 1728. He took an active part in rooting out the devil wherever he thought that he was lurking. Mather destroyed a lot (some say hundreds) of people he believed to be witches. Not to move against witchcraft would, to him, have been betraying Christ.

Reverend Mather established regular communications with the Deity and received encouragements only he could understand. He entered states of rapture through fasting, lonely vigils, and self-mortifications which allowed him to talk directly with God. At times he delivered himself out-of-body, to the heavens.

In the Reverend Mather's diary, he tells about his numerous conversations with the spirits and with God. The following is from an entry dated June 6, 1702: ". . . while I was at prayer with my dying wife, in her chamber, I began to feel the blessed breezes of a particular Faith, blowing from Heaven upon my mind. I thought I received an assurance from Heaven, that she should recover." She never did recover in this life.

Another eyewitness to the existence of the Other Side was Joseph Smith, Jr. During a spring morning in 1820, he was in the woods praying vocally. An evil power came over him and attempted to destroy him. Smith called upon God to deliver him from the evil force.

"I saw a pillar of light exactly over my head, above the brightness of the sun, which descended gradually until it fell upon me. It no sooner appeared than I found myself delivered from the enemy which held me bound. When the light rested upon me I saw two Personages, whose brightness and glory defy all description, standing above me in the air."

Four years later Smith was visited by a heavenly being called Moroni, who told him about the location of gold plates which contained God's gospel. Another four years passed, and he began to translate the golden plates. That translation became the first edition (1830) of The Book of Mormon. The Prophet, Joseph Smith, Jr., went on to found the Church of Jesus Christ of Latter-day Saints.

Reverend Billy Graham has told us that he "has felt the

presence of the Lord.'' In *Angels* he writes: ''As an evangelist I have often felt far spent to minister from the pulpit to men and women who have filled stadiums to hear a message from the Lord. Yet again and again my weariness has vanished, and my strength has been renewed. I have been filled with God's power, not only in my soul but physically.'' God has become real to the Reverend Graham.

Professor J. H. M. Whiteman gives an account of his own religious experience in *The Mystical Life*. One night, Professor Whiteman became fully awake and immediately he separated from his body. His ''separated form was drawn upwards, quickly, as if through a great distance. . . . All at once, without any further change, my eyes were opened. Above and in front, yet in me, of me and around was the Glory of the Archetypal Light . . . a creative light of Life itself, streaming forth in Love and Understanding and forming all other lives out of its substance. . . .''

In inquiring into the nature of the Other Side for a knowledge of what the next world is like and for a better understanding of how to live this life, man has turned for help to formal religions. The various religions have sprung from just the kind of visionary incidents that shaped the behavior of Moses, Mather, Smith, and Graham. The experiences of individuals who have witnessed the next world and gleaned some understanding of that life have enabled them to restructure religious life in this world.

The founders of various religions have been witnesses to some sort of revelation. They have seen, heard, and/or experienced something unusual. When Moses saw the burning bush, he creatively saw the emergence of the religion of the Israelites. The God who appeared as a fire in the desert revealed to Moses the need for a new religious order. Religion springs mostly from a need to feel secure in the knowledge that life after death is assured, and people take that assurance from their visions.

Sir James George Frazer theorizes, in *The Golden Bough*, that civilizations are born out of religions and that religions come out of magic. Mana is a force in nature which seems magical to primitive peoples. The practice of killing animals became a ritual and birth was seen as magic. Sex was also looked upon as religion. Early man did not see good and evil. The concepts came later as man became more civilized.

Some time, about 50,000 years ago, in more than just an isolated instance or two, something did indeed happen to early man's attitude toward the dead and the hereafter.

Suddenly and mysteriously the human and semihuman dead of our very early ancestors were no longer dumped or left laying on top of the earth like a dead animal for the carrion to dispose of. Instead, they were ritualistically placed in sealed *enclosures* in the ground. A change in viewpoint and attitude occurred. Cultural anthropologists have been able to observe the change. Perhaps it had to do with the acquisition of a soul. Perhaps it was a sudden awareness of isolation and the subsequent loneliness that drove primitive men closer together in spirit than lower animals.

Men could no longer stand to be reminded of the end of his fellow man and he started covering the dead with the soil and rocks. Five millennia ago Neanderthal man started to bury the dead. At Le Moustier, a young Neanderthal boy was found in a trench. And most importantly, objects of his previous existence were placed alongside him. Flints were put under his head along with a perfect stone ax. Pieces of charred meat may have been left as food for the dead in their journeys.

Not far from the site of the boy's burial, another, more elaborate grave-site was found. The remains of three children and two adults were found in a kind of family plot.

How did early man suddenly and mysteriously come to their change in view concerning death and burial? Sixty-thousand-year-old remains reveal head wounds with smoothed ridges. Normally such a wound would result in death. But maybe one of the ancient men recovered and somehow expressed what he had seen on the Other Side.

A cult developed in which it was necessary to bury the dead with certain objects, to help them in their new world.

The Neanderthal man saw that the soul continued to exist in another world. The Neanderthal man also started to kill his fellowman in about the same time period that burial practices were developed. Religion began.

The Egyptians of long ago saw the afterlife as a noncorporeal existence in which the one who died was allowed to enjoy those things which were available on the earth. The Egyptians felt that the body had to be preserved so that the spirit could return and be brought back to life. They also believed that the spirit had to have items of comfort placed with his body so that when he came back he could use them. This idea increased the significance of the manner in which the dead were buried.

I made a telephone call to the Greek Orthodox Archdiocese to learn about the views of the hereafter of that sect. A Father told me about the joys that would be found in paradise.

"We receive our view of paradise from that which is

presented in the Old Testament of the Bible. I really don't define heaven or hell for that matter, because I really don't know if the Bible is painting a literal picture of the places.''

I inquired whether there was any specific idea of what the hereafter would be like.

''There is nothing specific. There will be joy in paradise for those who attain that state. I think that that joy is merely a higher plane of existence.''

''How does a member of the Greek Orthodox Church attain his future life?'' I wanted to know.

''It is a Christian-type hereafter. Christ is our personal savior. I believe that upon our death Christ will determine our behavior during life, and He will judge us from that. If you accept Christ and lead a Christian life, you will be welcomed into heaven.''

I asked the Father about the Greek Orthodox view on migration of the soul from the dead person's body.

''My church believes in the extension and the survival of the soul.''

This answer led me to ask, ''How about the ability to contact the departed?''

''I do not think that direct communication with those in the other world is possible. One cannot contact the spirits of the departed. Only through prayers to Christ will one be able to contact the next world and that will be accomplished most indirectly.''

So the Greek Orthodox view of the hereafter is not clear. They firmly believe in the existence of the Next World, but they do not like to draw pictures of what might be there.

According to the doctrine of Christian Scientists, our

behavior is judged hourly by God. We cannot contact the dead; there are no spirits, and no demons. According to the founder of the Christian Scientists, Mary Baker Eddy, heaven exists in one's mind.

"Heaven is not a locality, but a divine state of Mind in which all the manifestations of Mind are harmonious and immortal, because sin is not there. . . .

"As a tree falls, so it must lie.

"As death findeth mortal man, so shall he awake. As death findeth mortal man, so shall he be after death, until . . . growth shall effect the needed change."

I next contacted a priest at St. Patrick's cathedral in New York, and asked, "What do Roman Catholics think heaven will be like?"

"We believe as did Saint Paul. We travel by faith darkly, and then when we get there, we will see Him as He is. We will participate after death in sharing the Light. This is the symbol of life. We do not believe in the ability to see visions."

I explained my study: "There have been several hundred people who have died and have been resuscitated. When these individuals are revived, they tell of wonderful things that they perceived while dead. They have seen spirits of loved ones coming to get them to take them to the hereafter. They have left their bodies. They have enjoyed the death experience and are unhappy to have to come back to this life. What do you think about these incidents?"

"The Church does not accept that they were really dead. According to the Bible, Christ has the ability to resurrect the dead. It is spelled out clearly in the Bible, and the Church scholars have studied that subject. The individuals were not really dead. Their so-called experiences in the hereafter were merely hallucinations brought on by shock to the nervous system."

Then I continued: "Several individuals claim to be able to act as mediums and make contact with loved ones who have died. Do you believe that we can contact the spirits?"

"No. We have no ability to communicate with the dead."

I talked with several rabbis to learn about the Jewish view of the hereafter. I had great difficulty in determining any view at all concerning the next world from the Jewish viewpoint. I was told to go ahead and search for heaven and hell on my own.

"There are good reasons for investigating the hereafter. It will improve your knowledge. It may give you hope for the future."

I received about the same kind of answers from several rabbis. "Our view of the next world is not as clear as that of the Christians." And, "Call the New York Board of Rabbis." And, "I don't know. Why don't you write Yeshiva University, they would know."

Finally I contacted a Rabbi Belton, in Brooklyn, who gave me no information at all on the hereafter, but who supplied me with all the places I would need to look on my own to find out about the Jewish hereafter.

Rabbi Belton told me: "We have no knowledge of God. We have no knowledge of the hereafter. I am a poor source of views on the hereafter. I spent several years in the Budapest Ghetto during the Second World War. The Nazi atrocities I witnessed while I was there thoroughly shook my religious views. Please ask someone else about heaven and the hereafter.''

But Rabbi Belton was not really anxious to get rid of me. We talked for a long time on various aspects of the Jewish religion. He told me about Orthodox ways of doing things, about the Conservative manner, and he enlightened me, generally, on the Jewish way of life.

In all, Jews seem to be divided on what they believe about the next life. Some maintain that when death comes there is nothing that follows, nothing at all but six feet of soil, or, if one has been very good, twelve feet of soil.

In terms of religious doctrine, early Judaism placed emphasis on *this* life, as it is. There was no concept of the next life, the hereafter. Later Judaism placed more emphasis on the hereafter. But even then there was no description of heaven and hell. Resurrection was seen as God's prerogative and not man's concern.

During my talks with the religious leaders, I learned a fascinating piece of information. Emanuel Swedenborg (1688-1772) was a philosopher, religious writer, seer, scientist, and inventor, who claimed that he consistently walked in heaven and in hell. He had started a religious order based on his visions from missions to the next world. He practiced out-of-body travels to see the Other Side.

I contacted the New Church in New York City to determine if I could speak to the minister there about OOBE's and the religion of Swedenborg. The minister was not in, but his wife was. She told me that she was writing a book on the subject and that she knew as much, if not more, than her husband concerning the life and travels of Emanuel Swedenborg.

"We have a strong belief in the next world. If we live this life as one of the usefulness, our spiritual body will go directly to the next life," the minister's wife told me.

So I wanted to learn: "How do you know about the next life or the hereafter?"

"Through the scriptures as revealed by the writings of Swedenborg."

I asked her if she had ever communicated with the spirits of the dead in the hereafter.

"Yes. I have caught an occasional glimpse of ghosts. I perceived it as a flash of communication."

I asked the woman her explanation of why we live on this plane.

"The major purpose of life on earth is to make angels out of humans. We learn to be born again."

I asked: "Do you believe in the reports made by the clinically dead concerning travels out-of-body and their perceptions of the Other Side?"

"I do believe that one can die, see the next world, and return to tell about it. Swedenborg did it often."

Looking at the writings of Swedenborg, I came across the following accounts which are very similar to those I have heard from the near-dead and the clinically dead.

"I am well aware that many will say that no one can possibly speak with spirits and angels so long as he lives in the body; and many will say that it is all a fantasy, others that I relate such things in order to gain credence, and others will make other objections. But by all this I am not deterred, for I have seen, I have heard, I have felt." (From *Arcana Coelestia*.)

"Fundamentally, a man's life in these other worlds is based on what he really is. In the present world, a person explores, develops, and forms himself. We are quite capable of deceiving ourselves and others. [In heaven] we move toward the essential reality of their existence. Hence it is that when the body is separated from its spirit, which is called dying, the man still remains, and lives." (From *Heaven and Hell*.)

"[After death] it is believed that he will then be a soul, and the common idea of a soul is that it consists of something like ether or air, thus that it is a breath, such as a man breathes out when he dies. Yet the fact is that after death a man is none the less a man; and so fully is he a man that he does not know but that he is still living in the former world. He sees, hears and speaks. . . . Death is not an extinction but a continuation of life, and merely a transition from one state to another." (From *True Christian Religion*.)

Emanuel Swedenborg even predicted accurately the time of his own permanent death.

Throughout my talks with representatives of the different religions, I heard the idea that heaven is where God dwells. It is also where the 'saved' go in their afterlives. In the Old Testament, heaven was the place of the god of the Israelites. Later in Jewish thought and teachings, the idea was advanced that the righteous would be resurrected to live in heaven with God also.

It is my religious conviction that when the proper relationship is met between the cosmic power of God and the spirit of man, salvation in the hereafter will be assured.

One preacher I talked with told me, "When we turn to a source of our guidance, we are led by our need to know of our future. Look at the following from our Bible.

" 'Also another book was opened, which is the book of

life. And the dead were judged by what was written in the books, by what they had done. And the sea gave up the dead in it, Death and Hades gave up the dead in them, and they were all judged by what they had done. Then Death and Hades were thrown in the lake of fire. This is the second death, the lake of fire; and if any one's name was not found written in the book of life, he was thrown into the lake of fire.' [Revelation 20:12-15]

"The believer knows from this that his present life will set the tone and quality in the next one. It tells me what to expect if I don't follow Christ's teachings."

Religions thus become the guideposts for our journeys to the Other Side. Religions meet more than just spiritual needs, they help maintain psychological adjustments. Man needs a hope in an afterlife, something beyond this mere existence. Religion deals with transcendental reality. It is neither scientific nor magical. Religion is a way to gain an understanding of the existence beyond this life. Religion is a pathway to understanding and knowledge for the true believer. It gives psychological security when that believer is given hope in overcoming the fear of the unknown—death.

14
DOES THE OTHER SIDE EXIST?

"At first, dying by freezing is very unpleasant. The pain sort of creeps up on you slowly at first, then it gets worse and worse. Every time I tried to move my fingers or toes, I almost passed out from the pain which resulted. I soon discovered that it was much better to lie there without moving. At least it did not hurt as much.

"Then I felt myself getting warm. 'Warm?' I asked myself. It did not seem possible. But I felt just like I was inside and electric blanket in my bed. This feeling of elation came over me. I did a little dreaming before I realized that I was dying here in the snow. I am freezing to death, and I feel contented. I tried to get up and move around, but my arms and legs would not work.

"I felt good now. The world around me became a blue-white tunnel. I felt myself starting to move toward a glowing warm light. I heard voices and music. The music was like choral music. It was very nice and relaxing. I was dead, and I felt very good. I was floating through this light-blue universe."

The rescue squad found him not too far from his abandoned car. He was either dead or unconscious, they didn't know which. His eyes were open, he had no pulse, no breathing, and he was blue in color.

He was given artificial respiration and placed in a thermal blanket. He was carried to the hospital where he successfully recovered, except for a few missing toes and fingers which were lost to the sub-zero temperatures and thirty-mile-an-hour winds.

Once the man had recovered enough to talk, he told the physicians how it felt to freeze to death. One of the physicians later told me that he thought the man was hallucinating the experience. Was it the truth or a figment of the man's partially frozen mind?

Other victims of the cold tell similar stories about their freezing experiences. In a *Reader's Digest* article, Oystein Moldtad-Anderson describes how it felt for Stein Gabrielson to spend several days clinging to a life raft in Atlantic waters of sixty degrees. He thought to himself, "How pleasant it would be to stretch out in the raft and drift off to sleep." He did not do this because he would have died in a few hours. Stein thought, "Even if you freeze to death, there are worse ways to die." Almost everyone who comes very close to death by freezing says the same thing—"It's very nice to freeze to death."

Stein Gabrielson did not freeze to death, but he came very close to it.

Russell Noyes reports in *Omega* a woman who was caught in a stalled car one sub-zero night. She experienced intense pain at first. Then the pain gave way to comfort and warmth. "For a moment, I was one with the Universe. Time, space, and myself were one and the same." Then she awoke in the hospital.

Are these individuals only experiencing their own, self-generated hallucinations, or are they actually experiencing the hereafter. In an earlier chapter, Victor Solow told of his experiences while clinically dead. He said that he knew he was dead—there was no doubt in his mind at all. And he did not care if anyone believed him or not. Almost everyone I have interviewed on their experiences in the hereafter speaks with great certainty concerning the events. None seem anxious to prove their points to the rest of us. They take the stand that it did happen, and it is the other person's problem if they don't believe that there is another reality, another world beyond this one.

It may be impossible to separate reports of hallucinations from real glimpses of the Other Side. Hallucinations are "real" to the person who has them. He believes in their existence. What scientists need to search for is some common element in the reports of those experiences with clinical death, near-death accidents, visions on the death-beds, and out-of-body travel. If we can find common views of the next world which are brought about by a wide assortment of contacts with death, we will come closer to being able to prove there is something else besides this existence.

Almost none of the dying patients and few of the clinically dead told of seeing religious figures. We might think that after a lifetime of cultural indoctrination on religion the person would fantasize about those things during their last moments. Only in those cases where a spiritual transformation took place (Moses, Cotton, Mather, Joseph Smith, Jr., etc.) did religious personages present themselves to the subjects.

It is not difficult to find a reason why the just-dead were unable to see angels, God, Jesus, and other religious figures. They were just starting on their journeys and had not reached the level where they would become aware of the Deity. If God wants you to see him, he will let you know.

How can we gather a glimpse of the Other Side, short of committing suicide? Can the sciences help us understand another realm?

The sciences have brought about a different view of ourselves in relationship to the universe. The electromagnetic environment influences our thinking and behavior in subtle and subconscious ways. We know of and are aware of the world only because of our psysiology. We know because we are able to perceive sensations. Our senses react to energies and transform them into nerve impulses. On our electronic instruments, a neural impulse from the eye appears identical to one coming from the foot. It is not the frequency, amplitude, wave length, or intensity of the stimulus that distinguishes it from other stimuli. We know that our perception of the universe is due to some kind of sorting process that occurs in our brains. The difference between a baby's cry and a sunset over New Jersey lies in our heads. It is where the nerve fibers end that let us know where we are. Our brains seem to be permanently wired in. This gives us a suggestion that thoughts may be transferred from one mind to another with electromagnetic energy that by-passes the normal sensory system of the body and impinges directly upon a particular section of the brain.

Science by itself, cannot explain the feelings and perceptions of those who have been exposed to the transcendental world of the Other Side. The view brought back by survivors is one, generally, of joy, happiness, contentment, and pleasure. There are many common elements running through the stories. The hereafter is seen as another reality, to be reached by an altered state of perception, where fear does not exist.

The following notice was carried in the *London Daily News*. for January 15, 1858. It is the story of Admiral Francis Beaufort's near-death due to drowning in Portsmouth Harbor in 1795.

"Thought rose above thought with a rapidity of succession that is not only indescribable, but probably inconceivable by any one who has not himself been in a similar situation. The course of those thoughts I can even now in a great measure retrace—the event which had just taken place—the awkwardness that had produced it—the bustle it must have occasioned—the effect it would have on a most affectionate father—the manner in which he would disclose it to the rest of the family—and a thousand other circumstances minutely associated with home, were the first series of reflections that occurred. They took then a wider range—our last cruise—a former voyage, and ship wreck—my school—the progress I had made there, and the time I had misspent and even all my boyish pursuits and adventures. Thus, traveling backwards, every past incident of my life seemed to glance across my recollection in retrograde succession; not, however, in mere outline, as here stated, but the picture filled up with every minute and collateral feature. In short, the whole period of my existence seemed to be placed before me in a kind of panoramic review, and each act of it seemed to be accompanied by a consciousness of right or wrong, or by some reflection on its cause or its consequences; indeed, many trifling events which had been long forgotten then crowded into my imagination, and with the character of recent familiarity.''

Once the pressures of struggling are finished, the fear of dying by drowning is forgotten, and the person resigns himself to his death, an altered state of consciousness is reached and the person finds himself blissfully contented with the situation.

This state of happiness and resigned contentment is found in a story told by John M., a twenty-eight year old resident of Manhattan who was scuba diving with a friend in the Atlantic Ocean in 1966 when he over-extended himself and drowned.

"I ran out of air and had to try and swim back to the shore. Before I got there, I was carried under the water by the outgoing tide and I felt myself die.

"Everything went totally and completely black. I felt an intense sensation surge throughout my entire body. The pain of exhaustion was removed. I became totally free of the constraints of the physical body. My strange new form of existence felt so exhilarating that my spirits were lifted up and away.

"A great burden had been lifted from my body and I felt free to observe the situation that I was in.''

I asked, "Do you mean that you left your body and were able to watch it exert itself in the raging ocean waters?''

"I was spectatoring myself. . . . I was watching myself swim to shore. It was like having my alter ego viewing in a detached manner from a distance, from someplace else. While spectatoring myself drowning, I directed my consciousness upwards and saw the intense blueness of the sky above. I seemed to be intrigued by the variations of the cloud formations. They were drifting across the distinctly blue background. They were intense white against the intense blue of the sky behind them. Time seemed wiped out. I was floating somewhere away from my drowning body, watching the heavens above. The feeling I got from looking at the sky was very intense. I loved the feeling of seeing the universe around me in a different perspective.''

Then I asked, ''Weren't you a little distraught over the fact that you were sinking below the surface of the water? You had to keep your head above the water level in order to breathe. Didn't it frighten you that you were dying, or possibly already dead?''

''No. I was filled with happiness. I knew that as far as this spectatoring spirit of myself was concerned, the body floundering in the turgid waters below was already gone.''

I asked John M. if he had experienced visions of others nearby.

''I saw no visions. I was aware of only the intense colors of the sky above and the body in the waters below.''

I told John M. about Admiral Beaufort's panoramic vision. ''Did anything like this happen to you?''

''No part of my life flashed in front of me. My horizons of awareness were severely limited. Everything was black, very black. Only when I directed my attentions upwards was I able to perceive something other than the black. I also saw myself in the waters.''

I wanted to know how he got out of the situation.

''As I was contemplating the clouds and sky above, an indescribable sensation came to my mind. ''Save yourself.' I don't know the reason that I decided to save myself. I was contented and happy with the floating sensations. I felt good. I did not feel tired, nor did I feel any pain. But the thought came to me, 'Save yourself.'

"Like the director of a movie, I told my physical body, 'Don't panic. Swim. Don't panic.' "

John M. kept telling himself this over and over again, until he felt his right flipper drag across the sandy bottom of the sand bar which led onto the shore. His spirit somehow rejoined his physical body and he struggled toward the shore. A huge black wave hit him squarely in the face as he was struggling those last few tortuous feet to land.

"I don't know if at the time I was hit by that wave whether I was still dead, but it succeeded in knocking me back into that state where I perceived only blackness."

It is not likely that John was unconscious, for if he was he would not have any remembrances of the blackness. It is more likely that he was clinically dead and perceiving the world beyond through altered states of his consciousness.

"Later the physicians at the hospital told me that I was clinically dead when those strangers along the shore had gotten me to dry land. They had seen my body in the waters and had rushed out to help."

The physicians told John that he had had no respiration or heart beat.

"I had pieces of memory after dying that are pretty incomplete. The first one was of being on the beach with someone pushing on my chest and breathing into my mouth."

His next memory was of the ambulance ride. It was only a fragment of a hazy thought. Then he blacked out again.

He came to for a moment in the hospital bed and finally fell asleep.

"My memory of my death experience is vivid. The most striking thing was how pleasant the feelings were. Once I quit struggling and drifted from my water-logged body, I felt totally alive. Everything in the distance was black. But I did see the most vivid colors in the heavens above. I felt very free. Sort of like a wispy cloud that shoots from one place to another. I was liberated from the shackles of the physical body. I know that I was dead. For how long, I do not know. But there I was floating above my own dead body."

John elaborated on the experience of directing a body from a distance.

"Once I had decided that I should save that body, I kept saying, 'Don't panic. Don't panic' to it.

"As I directed its efforts to swim, I had no idea of direction in a physical sense. I did feel a sense of 'upness' but I did not really know which way the land was. I had no awareness of the tiredness of my physical body. I was not consciously aware of the physical efforts involved with swimming. It was as though I was totally separated from the physical, and was operating in the spiritual world."

Had there been any effects of this death experience that had carried over?

"I took a shower once at my parents house which had one of those pulsating showerheads in it. I had to get out from under it because I suddenly felt myself being swept under the tides and waters of the Atlantic Ocean. I thought I was drowning. It was a most unpleasant sensation."

(Physicians have been warning their patients with cardiac problems not to use those pulsating shower heads. It seems that in a few instances some people's hearts have been stopped by the impact of those jets of water striking their chests.)

I asked about other carry-over effects.

"About four months ago while I was at a meditation session, I started to choke. This choking sensation suddenly caused my thoughts to return to the drowning experience. It had been two years since the shower experience and two years since I had given the death experience any thought. Then here I was, at a meditation class, thinking that I was drowning in the ocean. There were about four or five people around me as I started choking and gagging. I consciously controlled the coughing and recovered very well.

"The other students did not know what to do. The teacher was shaken at what she had thought was my impending death.

"Later I told her that something important had happened to me during that experience. I discovered that I could consciously control the congestion and controlled my own body so I could breathe again.

"I can now control my own consciousness so that I can enter or leave the physical body. I left my body before as I was drowning. Now I can leave that body through meditation. My altered state of consciousness is a way to travel from my body."

The recognition of and the proof for the existence of another reality will ultimately rest with a person's altered state of consciousness which will allow him to visit, first-hand, that realm. There are several ways in which you can alter your perceptions. You can meditate, as John

M. does. You can experience death itself. You can have a near-death experience. You can dream about it.

The source of a person's inner psychic dispositions are his dreams. Carl Gustav Jung was a psychiatrist who believed that dreams proved the existence of the hereafter. In *Man and His Symbols* Jung writes: "People feel that it makes a great difference if only they had a positive belief . . . in God and immortality. The specter of approaching death often gives a powerful incentive to such thoughts. From time immemorial men have had ideas about . . . the Land of the Hereafter." Since scientists cannot discover it with their telescopes and microscopes, many don't believe in its existence. The idea of Other Side is seen as false. Jung feels that there must be something to the idea of the Next World since those kind of ideas have been around since prehistoric times "and they still break through into consciousness at any provocation." The denial of the existence of the hereafter is as impossible to "prove" as is its existence. For Jung the collective unconscious thought of the human race is proof enough for him to accept the idea of the hereafter. He feels that the belief in the Next World which is held by so many individuals in the world as a primary element in religion and which is the subject of innumerable dreams should not be dismissed as being unscientific and false. Jung believes that this idea must be based upon fact and not on myth.

Dreams are our link with the hereafter. Dreams are our window to the Other Side. The altered state of consciousness found in a dreaming state is a better source of information on death than are "scientific approaches" to understanding.

According to Dr. John Palmer, of the University of

California at Davis, out-of-body experiences (OOBE's) are related to dream states. In his April 1974 article for the *Osteopathic Physician*, Dr. Palmer describes OOBE's. "Under what might be labeled normal states of being, OOBE's tend to occur most frequently when a person is either in the light stage of sleep or on the verge of sleep, what dream researchers call the hypnagogic period." Images in dreams occur during this light period of sleep and these images may derive from travels from the body. "Some persons who have reported the ability to induce OOBE's voluntarily in themselves suggest techniques whereby one becomes aware during a dream that he is dreaming (i.e., a 'lucid' dream) and then turns this into an OOBE. Indeed, OOBE's are often difficult to distinguish from lucid dreams."

Emanuel Swedenborg was able to travel to heaven and hell by practicing OOBE's while in light sleep states. Using meditation, Swedenborg soared out of his body and traveled to new levels of consciousness. What had started for Swedenborg as intellectual meditation broadened into psychic journeys.

Swedenborg writes in *World Explained*, "Another vision is that between the time of sleep and the time of wakefulness, when the man is waking up, and has not yet shaken off sleep from his eyes. This is the sweetest of all, for heaven then operates into his rational mind in the utmost tranquility."

Bob Monroe, the teacher of OOBE techniques, believes that almost everyone can be taught to leave their physical bodies in varying degrees of completeness during dreaming. Relaxation, self-hypnosis, and the ability to let the mind drift freely are Monroe's ways of accomplishing his journey out of his body to the Other Side.

Once, while out-of-body, Monroe came to a boy in spirit-form who was alone and frightened. ''I told him to wait right where he was, that some friends of his would be along shortly, that they would take him where he was supposed to go.'' The next day Monroe read about the death of a young boy who had died about the same time Monroe had told the spirit of a boy that friends would soon come along to get him.

The Other Side awaits all of us. Some have visited for a short time and have returned to tell us of the joys and peacefulness in the hereafter. Some are now practicing ways to go and see the next world. The Other Side does exist and it will be everything that we want it to be.

15
THE JOY OF DEATH

"Death has replaced sex as the forbidden subject," wrote Malcolm Muggeridge in *The Observer* (February 20, 1970). The topic of death is pornographic to some and saddening to most.

But it is not unpleasant to those who have made that journey. "Being dead for that moment was the most pleasurable thing that has ever happened to me. The sensations were beautiful," said one recently resuscitated woman. Her view of death changed as a result of her experience on the Other Side. She believes that true, unbounded happiness awaits her death. She is not frightened.

Even those who die while suffering from severe pain tell about the joy they found in death.

"It was a tremendous feeling to die. A good feeling. I was in a lot of pain. Then I felt myself drifting away from the pain. I think I died. As I died, I felt good. I saw myself on the operating table. The doctors were frantically trying to bring me back, but I did not want to come back. I drifted farther and farther away. I saw the void of the universe, and I saw the spirits of some of my dead friends. They seemed to be coming toward me. I was about to join them when I was slammed back into this world. I felt the sickening pain again.''

This speaker was telling me about his experience while dead. In fact, he had died three times and was resuscitated three times before the doctors could finish removing the two bullets from his body. Notice that the person's perception of the Other Side is filled with good memories even though he was suffering from two nearly fatal bullet wounds. The pains of this life are changed into something marvelous in the hereafter. This is true regardless of the kind of death—whether violent or peaceful.

Our attitudes toward the Other Side are being changed by those who have made a round-trip visit to the next world. They have come back telling us about the wonders and joys in the hereafter. Almost all say that they did not want to come back to this life.

Our society teaches us to fear dying and to close our eyes to death. We have been taught that dying is ugly. In our literature and arts, death and the hereafter are presented in bleak and somber perspectives. Writers of death conjure up the worst of feelings and emotions. Edgar Allen Poe writes about our worst fears in his story, ''The Premature Burial.'' ''So far, I had not ventured to stir any of my limbs—but now I violently threw up my arms, which had been laying at length, with the wrists crossed. They struck a solid wooden substance, which extended above my person at an elevation of not more than six inches from my face. I could no longer doubt that I reposed within a coffin at last.''

People fear dying a slow, painful death. Edgar Allen Poe was one individual whose relationships with dying and death altered his view toward life. All of the women he loved in life died. His writings reflect his experiences as well as one of the more terrifying aspects of death, that of premature burials. Poe is but one of several authors who have succeeded in painting an awful picture of the events leading to death.

A Colonel Townsend of England went into a form of suspended animation while being watched by Dr. G. Cheyne. Townsend was clinically dead for half an hour, with no respiration or heartbeat. In W. R. Hadwen's book, *Premature Burial*, published in 1905, these trancelike states are described as being fashionable for people of that day to engage in.

After my experience with dying, my interviews with others who have been clinically dead, and reading the accounts of others who have shared experiences with death similar to mine, I have come to the conclusion that one can expect death to bring a spiritual expansion and a becoming one with the universe. There is nothing to fear about the Other Side and, in fact, many who have seen it now exclaim about the joys and happiness of death.

The research done by Dr. Elisabeth Kubler-Ross has begun to reshape the prevailing negative and depressing views toward the Other Side. Attitudes of promise and optimism are emerging. In *On Death and Dying* Dr. Kubler-Ross explains how physicians were at first reluctant to tell patients about forthcoming death. The terminally ill were never supposed to know of their impending deaths. Dying was a topic which patients were not to hear about.

But those who are dying should know about their approaching deaths so that they can prepare themselves spiritually. According to the Christian view, to die unprepared is the worst misfortune that can happen.

Dr. Kubler-Ross wanted to set up talks with the terminally ill at a certain hospital so they could be forewarned and prepared for their deaths. At first the hospital staff was hostile to the idea of seminars held to discuss the process of dying and the hereafter. It was felt that the subject would cause psychological injury to dying patients. But, after a time, the physicians and staff learned that the patients did not get upset when the facts were presented to them. The terminally ill demonstrated great insights and awareness concerning their illnesses. They were able to handle it better than their doctors.

The reason for attempting to prove the patients' views toward dying is presented in *On Death and Dying*. "To live on borrowed time, to wait in vain for the doctors to make rounds, lingering on from visiting hours to visiting hours, looking out of the window . . . is the way many terminally ill patients pass their time."

After the series of lectures on the hereafter, a positive change in attitude occurred in patients and hospital staff. An improved view of the Other Side emerged.

Patients want to know about their forthcoming death. They can sense their fate even though the doctors do not tell them. It is cruel not to help them approach death with a positive attitude.

Partly from the work of scientists like Dr. Kubler-Ross, partly as a result of the reports made by the clinically dead, and partly for humanitarian reasons, the hospital environment for the terminally ill is being drastically improved. How we view death shapes the way we react to it.

Joan Kron described a new development in terminally-ill-patient care in *New York Magazine*. An environment has been designed to smooth the troubled emotions of the dying and their friends who visit them.

In hospitals, death comes in a sterile environment. There is no joy, no laughter, no warmth—only loneliness for the dying and despair by the living.

A proposed New Haven hospital has been designed for patients without much time left. The patients can bring with them to the hospital things which please them. The dying are not kept from the living. It is a place for waiting for death when everything else has been done. Research has shown that patients and their families would prefer this kind of hospital—one where they can be together in warm living surroundings. There is a design book, *The Hospital: A Social and Architectural History*, written by consultant John Thompson, showing buildings where death can be awaited when life is almost finished.

Dr. Cicely Saunders established St. Christopher's Hospital in London. In this hospital, families are kept from the intensive care units, but they are invited to the deathbed areas with open arms. The reality of death is part of everyone's consciousness.

Other effects of a changing attitude toward death can be seen in the educational and religious programs that are being revamped in various locations throughout the nation. The Office of Religious Education in the Diocese of Trenton has established a new Thanatology Department. The educational program is designed to change people's fears of death. The afterlife is explored and practical suggestions shared and offered through lectures.

Where death was once a taboo topic, scarcely discussed, now universities are offering courses on death.

The progressive and innovative New School of Social Research in New York City offers a course for adults who are interested in death. The course is called "The Philosophy and Psychology of Death." The school brochure describes the course as: "A discussion of various philosophical and psychological questions about death with special reference to the theories of the existentialists and to contemporary psychological research on human attitudes towards death. The following topics are included: the mind-body problem . . . immortality . . . all men must die alone . . . the fear of death . . . all fears are really fears of death . . . Does belief in an afterlife relieve anxiety?"

Several religious cults have sprung up which tell about the glories of the hereafter in terms very similar to those of the ancient Indian legends.

Long before the white man arrived in the Americas, Indian legends told about a mysterious white person who wandered about the plains of America telling the Indians about the next world. This man, according to the legends, had a beard, copper-colored hair, and a long, flowing robe. He wore sandals of gold. In L. Taylor's book, *He Walked the Americas*, this preacher of the hereafter had a strange radiance, "each hair on his head luminescent, his garments glowing."

There are cults which believe that flying saucers represent visitors from the land of the once-thought-to-be dead. God and the other religious personages are seen as being extraterrestrials. Members of these cults firmly believe that Jesus was an astronaut from another realm. Even the angels are pictured as travelers from the Other Side.

R. L. Dione wrote *God Drives a Flying Saucer* in

which he presented not theory, but hard facts that "flying-saucer occupants are responsible for the scriptures, prophecies and miracles of the Christian religions." In *God and Spacemen of the Ancient Past* W. Raymond Drake writes that Jesus Christ was a great intelligence from a higher place, incarnated on earth to inspire man's spiritual evolution. Drake told how spacemen mated with earthwomen to produce a mutation.

Gerard R. Steinhauser writes, in *Jesus Christ: Heir to the Astronauts*, that early man's perceptions of the hereafter were probably shaped by the early astronauts who visited the earth tens of thousands of years ago. Steinhauser says: "How would it be possible for people to talk and dream of paradise (and also of evil and unfriendly worlds) unless someone had described such places to them or perhaps even taken them there?"

A recent cult which promises the riches of paradise to its believers is being led by Marshall Applewhite of Spur, Texas, accompanied by Ms. Bonnie Lue Nettles. These two have been able to convince people in California, Arizona, Texas, Nebraska, and Oregon to give up their worldly possessions and abstain from sexual activities while they wait to be taken to the hereafter by a flying saucer. Applewhite and Nettles claim that they came from the "world of Jesus," who, according to brochure distributed by the faithful, "left the earth in a flying saucer" and will return to pick them up.

The Egyptians once thought that the body was the temple for the soul. The body must be preserved so that the traveling spirit can return. But changing attitudes toward death and the hereafter are changing our view toward the way we bury our dead.

Once, when life was simple, the dead were buried quickly in a nearby churchyard. As towns became cities, graveyards were placed further away, outside the city.

The American Civil War made it necessary to satisfy the emotional needs of the living. The government just could not bury a mother's only son in an unmarked grave in a field in Georgia. She had to see him for that last time so she could cry and he would know she had cared. Embalming processes were borrowed from the ancient Egyptians so that that son's body could be preserved. We now embalm the dead for health reasons.

In 1959 at a National Funeral Directors Association gathering, Robert Fulton discussed the religious significance of the funeral industry. Catholics viewed the funeral ceremony as being for the dead person's spirit. Protestants saw the funeral in terms of pacifying the emotions of the living—a comfort to the family in "Their time of need."

Inexpensive burials are a new trend.

In California and New York, firms will cremate the body and toss the ashes into the sea. A California company called Telophase registers individuals for $25 ($15 for senior citizens). It picks up the dead body in a station-wagon for delivery to a licensed crematory. The ashes are disposed of at sea. The bill to the survivors is about $300. Many people are now opting for this method of burial.

Jacqueline Susann's ashes are kept in a bronzed book between her bestsellers *Valley of the Dolls* and *The Love Machine*.

The Society for Perpendicular Interment has advocated a dramatic change in burial practices. The Society's view is that "the dead take up too much room and should be buried standing up and close together."

All this is evidence that as more proof has been offered for the existence of the human spirit and survival as something separate from the physical body, feelings of horror about death are changing.

16
THE SPIRIT WORLD

"Oh, spirit of the hereafter, can you hear me? If you can understand me, please indicate by knocking with the table."

Then, as if by some unseen force in the universe beyond, one side of the card table lifted a couple of inches off the tile floor. There we were, four college-educated people seated around a folding table, lightly touching its surface while it reared with two legs off the floor. The instigator of the séance was Mickey S., who was my business acquaintance.

"Guiding spirit of the hereafter, we need your help in solving a problem. Are you the spirit of the next world? If yes, knock once. No, knock twice."

The table banged the floor once.

We asked the spirit of the table several mundane questions and then got to the heart of the séance. "Will the price of frozen pork bellies go up in June?"

It was a question of major importance since Mickey was

investing most of my life savings in the commodity futures market. I didn't want any mistakes. Needless to say, the June pork belly market didn't respond as the spirit indicated it would, and I lost my money.

This example is but one of many where individuals claim to be able to contact someone or something in the next world. My medium, Mickey, just happened to use a table to allegedly get to the Other Side.

Spiritualists claim that through mental powers they are able to contact the Other Side. Usually a spirit guide is needed to aid in the process. But the mediums who talk to the dead are at best controversial and at worst completely fraudulent. Contacting the spirits can be a profitable business.

Harry Houdini, the famed magician, was never able to recover psychologically from the death of his beloved mother. He spent long months after her death trying to determine if she had made it to the Other Side. Houdini was a personal friend of Sir Arthur Conan Doyle, and Houdini asked Doyle's wife to arrange a séance with Arthur Ford, a psychic and sensitive.

During the séance, a spirit appeared and spoke, ''Dear Harry, I'm at peace here. I am very happy. . . .'' Houdini couldn't control his anger. He felt that the séance was a hoax, and he recognized it immediately.

Harry Houdini later told reporters, ''My real name is Eric Weis. Mamma called me Eric. The so-called spirit spoke English, but my mamma spoke only German and English.''

Houdini spent the rest of his life attempting to debunk all mediums and other false communicators with the spirit world. He put up a $2500 reward in *Scientific American* for any message, apparition, or psychic phenomena that he could not reproduce. A reward of $100,000 is now offered for proof of the spirit world.

In 1967, Episcopal Bishop James Pike went on Canadian television to communicate with his son who had committed suicide in 1965. In a séance, Pike was contacted by his deceased son. The information Pike received from the Other Side was too private for other people to have known and Reverend Pike was convinced that the spirit of his son had communicated with him.

Back at home, strange things happened to Pike. Clocks stopped running at 8:19, which was the time that Pike's son had died. Postcards from the boy turned up on tables and chairs. Pike could not separate truth from hullucination in these matters. He did not know if he was dreaming or if his son was contacting him.

Pike attended another séance, one especially established by Arthur Ford, a well-known medium and investigator of the spirit world, in which proof of the existence of the Other Side was shown once again.

James A. Pike wrote *The Other Side: An Account of My Experience with Psychic Phenomena*. "What can I really believe about life after death?" Pike asked. His book concerned experiences involving his son, Jim, who was attempting to communicate with him even though he was dead.

Pike told Phyllis Battelle, a syndicated columnist, that he was able to talk to his son through spiritual mediums, but that he was still "not sure of what lay in the beyond."

Bishop Pike searched for and finally was reunited with his son. They found his body in the Sinai desert.

The strangest cases of the dead contacting the living involve dreams.

The *Proceedings of the Society for Psychical Research*

carried a story told by Mrs. Henry Sidgwick about a man who had had a dream in which another person appeared and told that he had not been guilty of killing himself.

According to the man, he went to sleep and the spirit appeared to him. "I cannot call it a dream; but let me use the common phraseology. I dreamt, but with no vagueness as in common dreams, no blurring of outline or rapid passages from one thing disconnectedly to another. Towards me, in front, advanced Robert Mackenzie. I was struck by the peculiar bluish-pale colour, and on his forehead appeared spots which seemed like blots of sweat."

Mackenzie reportedly told the dreaming man, "I am innocent. I did not do the thing they say I did."

Later it was discovered that Mackenzie had mistakenly drunk some wood-staining liquid, believing it was whiskey. He died an agonizing death, but he did not do it on purpose.

Dr. Hornell Hart, professor of sociology at Duke University, thought that some people could consciously project their spiritual beings to other locations where others have reported seeing apparitions. *The Enigma of Survival*, by Dr. Hart, is an attempt to show that conscious apparitions of the living are just like those of the dead and, therefore, offer some evidence of spiritual survival.

Dr. Robert Van de Castle is director of the Sleep Laboratory at the University of Virginia. He believes that he has found proof that the spirits of the dead are able to communicate through extrasensory channels with the living. A rich North Carolina man who had died returned to one of his four sons as a vision in a dream. He kept pointing to the raincoat that he was wearing. Upon waking, the son located that raincoat and looked in the pocket that his father had been pointing to in the dream. In his pocket the son found a will that his father must have completed just before dying. The will indicated that the father had had a change of mind and had decided that he would name all four sons as beneficiaries of his estate, instead of just the one.

It seems that the world of spirits is opened to those about to die. Dr. Charles Garfield of the University of California's Medical Center told how a pain-racked woman suddenly felt no pain. She told Dr. Garfield that her mother was expecting her to join her in the hereafter. The pain left the woman and she died quite peacefully a few minutes later.

Those scientists and researchers who explore the far out areas of psychic phenomena—clairvoyance, precognition, psychokinesis, spiritualism, and other areas of parapsychology—have done much in showing that there is a survival of the soul after bodily death.

According to Gardner Murphy, author of *Challenge of Psychical Research*, paranormal events can be explained in terms of spiritual forces. "For many people, every telepathic event is ultimately a transaction in which unseen spiritual entities assist in the communion between the living. For others, the very fact that such things as telepathy can exist is taken to mean the reality of a spiritual order."

Parapsychology is a very recently developed scientific discipline. But parapsychological experimentation has produced amazing results. Telepathy has been shown to exist. Perception of events outside the normal range of human experiences has been demonstrated in several studies.

Parapsychology includes the study of extrasensory perception and telepathy. Various scientific experiments have shown that some people in some instances do possess extraordinary powers, such as the strange ability to read the thoughts of others. Some researchers believe that communications with the spirits of the dead are possible.

Mental telepathy is a serious subject in several leading universities, government labs, and private organizations.

During his Apollo 14 flight, astronaut Edgar Mitchell, attempted to telepathetically send visual symbols to four individuals on earth who were psychically gifted. The results were checked when Mitchell arrived back on earth and were found to have some notable accuracy. Mystical and transcendental experiences of outer space may have caused Mitchell to understand more of the "universal truth" of the universe.

Mitchell decided to establish a scientific organization that would have as its purpose the study of psi. The Institute of Noetic Sciences was established in California to foster the application of parapsychology for useful purposes.

One of the first scientists to study telepathy was Dr. J. B. Rhine, of Duke University. His interest in the paranormal started when he was a boy in the mountains of Pennsylvania. There he heard many stories involving "psychic" things which involved gathering information in ways other than through the normal senses. In *New Frontiers of the Mind*, Dr. Rhine describes how he became interested in the field of parapsychology. While attending a university, a professor told Rhine about an incident which caught his undivided attention because it seemed to prove to this skeptical scientist that telepathy did exist. The professor told about a neighbor who had dreamed about her brother whom she thought had gone up into the haymow and shot himself with a pistol. She awoke everyone in the house to tell the story. She was adamant that they finally hitched the buggy and went into town. When they got to town, they did find her brother exactly as she had dreamed it.

Dr. Rhine described his reaction to the story as a lasting one which set the tone for his investigations into the world of telepathic communications. The professor's "story" puzzled and impressed me when I heard it, and it has remained in my mind long years after most of the things he taught in class have been forgotten. It is not the story alone that I have remembered, but the fact that the man who told it, himself a teacher and a scientist, though clearly impressed by the occurrence, had no explanation whatever to offer."

Louisa E. Rhine is co-founder with her husband, J. B. Rhine, of the first American laboratory for studying psychic things in a scientific manner. In her book, *Psi: What Is It?*, Mrs. Rhine devotes three chapters to the psi experiences involving life after death.

Louisa Rhine describes one area of investigation which offers some proof of the survival of the soul, "Experiences in which a dead person seems to bring a message to a living one have occurred many times and in many different forms over the years. Also, instances have been reported involving a person not already known to be dead, but who, as it proved, was dying at the time." In one instance, a 13-year-old girl was "visited" by her grandmother. The grandmother appeared at the doorway and told the girl not to worry because she was going on a short trip. When her parents returned home the girl told them, "Mommy, Grandma came to see me while you were away."

"You must have been dreaming. Grandma died tonight. She's gone, dear."

Parapsychologists believe that modern psychics can explain the nature of the Other Side. Spirits only exist in terms of another dimension. The discovery of the 100 fundamental particles has strengthened this kind of thinking. Hadrons are viewed as massless strings of things whose ends move with the speed of light in several dimensions.

Physicists have pushed our understanding of subatomic particles into the realm of metaphysics and parapsychology. They have found particles, called neutrinos, which seems to move backward in time. These particles have no charge, no mass, and the ability to penetrate the entire earth at the speed of light without running into any of the earth's atoms.

Neutrinos are at the fringes of science and at the boundaries of the hereafter. They do not behave as they should. They do not conform to "natural law" as defined by psysicists. The particles have minds of their own. Physicists label them "quarks" and say they possess "charm." They are ghostlike things with transitory existences in this world.

Just as all matter has as its counterpart antimatter, the universe may also have its counterpart—an antiuniverse of the spirits and souls.

Arthur Koestler relates extrasensory perception and modern physics in his book, *The Roots of Coincidence*. "On both the cosmic and the sub-atomic scale this intimate, tangible relationship turns out to be an illusion." There are those who can see the shadows of the spirits. It would be easy enough to ascribe those perceptions into categories of hallucinations if it were not for the predictability of the seer's visions.

"I see shadows of things just before deaths in my family. Once while I was knitting, I saw a shadow crossing from one side of the room to the other. I called my sister and told her I was worried about something happening to a member of the family."

The lady I interviewed believed that shadows indicated potential trouble for some member of the family. She had some difficulty describing what the shadows looked like, but she knew they foretold of future disaster.

"I did not know what was going to happen to us, but I kept seeing this shadow. Then I fell and fractured my leg. Two days later the shadow returned and I fell again and fractured my arm this time."

I asked her about the relationship between the shadow and deaths in the family.

"Several times I have seen the shadow and several times there have been deaths of people I have known, usually members of the family. Several years ago I saw a shadow quite distinctly. My husband died within two weeks of the time that I saw the shadow."

"I saw the shadows just before my young cousins died in an accident. I saw a shadow coming toward the house and my aunt died very soon thereafter. I always see that shadow when death approaches."

"Seeing these shadows started when I was a child. I once saw my little girlfriend, Irene. She was floating from wall to wall in my room. This was years ago when almost everyone had horse and buggys. The day after I saw Irene's shadow floating in my room she was run over and killed by a horse and buggy.''

''I'm a nurse. I see the shadows when a patient is on the verge of death. I see the shadow and the patient dies. The other nurses call me a witch because I can predict to the hour the time which they will die.''

We talked for a long time concerning her ability to see the approach of death. She did not seem especially worried about her ability to see into the future. She considered her predictive ability as merely an intuitive ability to understand death better than those around her.

A friend of mine had to work late one night and she could not take her mother to see the opera ''Aida.'' Since the tickets had been purchased I offered to take her mother while she worked. On the way to the opera I had a chance to talk with her concerning something she had felt brush by her as she sat next to the bedside of her dying husband.

''Many years ago my husband suffered a heart attack and was admitted to the hospital. I was standing outside his room when the nurse yelled out to me to grab hold of my husband's hand. As I did so he raised his head, smiled, and said to me, 'I think I see Mother.' And then I felt and heard something like a whirr and a breeze go by me.''

Mrs. J. was pregnant with Norma at the time of Mr. J's heart attack. Although he lived for eight days after the passage of the breeze-like shadow, the doctor confided to the family that Mr. J. was a ''sour patient''—a person destined to die within a short time.

''During the last night that Mr. J. was alive I heard my husband moan much like a sick cow.''

"My husband whispered to me on that last night, 'I see Mother.' He was talking about his mother who had died several years before this. He asked me: 'Are you going to be all right?' I said I would be all right. He asked the nurse if I was going to be all right. She told him that I would be okay. 'I can't go on any longer.' The atmosphere got heavier after midnight. My husband died within the hour after midnight. He was only 38 years old."

"Did you feel anything when he died?"

"I was only conscious of a nice sound at that time."

Can the living see the shadows of the departed spirits? Peter Mosca of Farmingville, New York believes that he can see certain spirits.

"I've seen my father-in-law in the form of a spirit after his death. The spirit was so life-like that I thought it was my father-in-law in spirit."

Mr. Mosca told me about something which happened to his brother-in-law. While he was dying, a picture of a bearded Saint appeared on his arm. When the brother-in-law passed away, the picture also went.

John Palmer of the University of Virginia's Medical School—the division of parapsychology—wrote an article "Some recent trends in Survival Research," *Parapsychology Research* (May-June, 1975) in which he discusses the qualitative differences of the things seen by persons claiming contact with the dead and those things produced by extrasensory perception subjects. Some individuals claim that spirits from the Other Side "drop-in" on them. Some researchers view these "drop-in" reports from mediums as supporting survival theories, especially those involving out-of-body travels and experiences.

The area of parapsychology comprising the spirit world

is indeed an interesting one, but looking at these things from a historical perceptive we find a considerable amount of fraud. Everyone so wants to believe their departed loved ones can be reached that they become easy marks for confidence games of individuals claiming the ability to contact the Other Side. Seeker beware!

17
THE OTHER SIDE

The Other Side does exist.

Much of the evidence for the existence for a hereafter is found in the reports of the individuals who have been temporarily dead, and then been resuscitated. Even without their reports, the difference between the living and the dead has never been very great. Everyone will make their own journey to the Other Side.

There have been, of course, many attempts to verify whether a body is dead or just in an unconscious state. In *King Lear*, Shakespeare described one of the more common, but fallible, methods of the day that was used to determine whether Cordelia was alive. "Lend me a looking glass; if her breath will mist or stain the stone, why, then she lives." Had present day patients who were clinically dead been tested with the looking glass, none would be alive today.

The medical authorities have attempted to define death exactly. It is embarrassing to pronounce someone dead and then have them come back to life spontaneously. It's okay to medically resuscitate someone. There is a difference. Another reason for attempting to define when someone is irreversibly dead so that a vegetable will not be kept alive. It is cruel to prolong the physical life of someone who has suffered complete and everlasting brain damage.

The Harvard Medical School established a committee, headed by Dr. Henry K. Beecher, to clearly define death. In the committee's report of 1968, it was concluded that the old definitions of death were no longer useful. "From ancient times down to the recent past it was clear that, when the respiration and heart stopped, the brain would die in a few minutes; so the obvious criterion of no heart beat as synonymous with death was sufficiently accurate."

The attitudes we have held for centuries about the finality of bodily death are changing due in part to the rapid advances in medical science technology. According to Dr. Beecher's final report in the *Journal of the American Medical Association* (1968), "when expert teams of physicians and technicians work together with the newest life supportive equipment they can now restore 'life' as judged by the ancient standards of persistent and continuing heart beat." Bringing life to a 'dead' body can be accomplished even though there is no possibility of the person ever being a conscious, thinking entity again.

But those who have briefly died do tell us that there is something in the next world which is good and that they would like to return to. If my experience with the Other Side taught me anything, it is that we should listen to and believe those reports.

Victor Solow died and came to the hereafter in a glorious way. The experience was something which made a lasting impression on Solow. His attitude on life changed as a result of what he experienced. When he died his soul sped away at great speed toward a universe totally different from the world he left. His spirit came into a pulsating grid, and he emerged from it as just an essence of what his former self had been. It was a good experience.

When Mary A. of Pennsylvania died she was commanded by God to return until it was time for her to return to the Other Side. She perceived the Other Side as a void without any noises or sights.

It is not only from those who have experienced clinical death that the Other Side's existence is revealed, but also we receive virtually the same picture from those who have come very close to certain death. In both instances, people have reported leaving their bodies, travelling through tunnels at rapid speeds, floating sensations, and a separation from the constraints of their physical bodies.

Scientists have been very skeptical of the reports made by people claiming to have seen the wonders of the next life. What little evidence we have for the existence of the Other Side has come from individuals which, historically, society has labeled as "queer," "looney," "schizophrenic," "insane," or "religious fanatics."

Researchers in the hard sciences, like physics, chemistry, and biology, require more objective proof for heaven and hell than is found in the verbal reports of what is seen as an emotionally upset individual. In the softer sciences, like psychology and sociology, reports of visits to another realm are viewed as legitimate sources of information to label a person "abnormal." This evidence is used by psychologists and psychiatrists to help the person come to the understanding that those things which he saw on the Other Side were only figments of his imagination and not of any real exposure to another existence. Man does not see heaven or hell except in the deep, dark recesses of his unconscious. Thinkers in the areas of mental inquiry, religion and philosophy, generally accept the idea of a continued existence of the human soul or spirit in another realm than this one and in another form than our physical bodies. It is in these areas that proof of the existence for life after death is accepted as a "leap of faith." If you believe a certain way, then you accept what that religious teaching offers. It is an internal feeling that comes to the believers; they can not prove it to someone else, but it truly exists for them.

Patricia Garfield, Ph.D., describes this "inner knowing" in her book, *Creative Dreaming* (Simon and Schuster, 1974). When you dream you know it. Trying to convince someone else that you saw this or that while you were asleep can only be done if the other person takes a "leap of faith" and believes what you tell them. Visiting the Other Side in your dreams "is rather like believing in the possibility of love; if you have never experienced it, it is difficult to believe it can exist for you. Once love has become a reality for you, no cynic on earth can persuade you that it does not exist."

A person who has been clinically dead and resuscitated may have had experiences while "dead" that may be just as real to them as those feelings of a person in love. In either case, the feelings and experiences might be difficult to explain and to share with others.

Scientists may say, "The so-called experiences of the clinically dead are the physiological and neurological reactions caused by the biological trauma induced by death. These experiences while dead are merely illusions or hallucinations.''

But on the other hand the mystical experiences may reflect actual visits to the hereafter. It is quite possible that the altered states of consciousness brought about by clinical death may allow for the utilization of hidden processes of the mind which are normally masked by the normal five senses. Once the person's channels of communication with the physical world are severed (temporarily or permanently), alternative pathways my cause the spirit to depart and travel to the Other Side.

Skeptics need more than just a story to convince them that there is something more after this life. They accept as factual the explanations that someone who is thought to be dead can be resuscitated or revived but stories do not prove or disprove anything.

One such story about an individual who died and then came back to life is found in a collection of Indian myths called *Yaqui Myths and Legends*. The stories were collected by Ruth Giddings and published by the University of Arizona in 1959.

"One time I sowed lots of corn and beans and squashes, many, many squashes. I fell sick. But I wasn't sick for very long, because I died! Soon all the important people gathered to attend my funeral. They made great fires and began to cook squashes all night long. And it is absolutely true. Those people finished every single squash. When they were about to bury me, I noticed that there were no more squashes, so I revived.''

When sane, and normal people suddenly ''hear'' voices, is it because they are being communicated with by the aliens from other worlds, or spirits from the Other Side?

Voices from other worlds told a man in Italy to take a hammer and beat on Michelangelo's sculpture the *Pieta*, in St. Peter's Rome. A voice told another man that he must slash Rembrandt's *Night Watch* in Amsterdam.

Well-educated and supposedly sane people are beginning to hear voices telling them to become an agent for the Lord. The events found in the Bible are thought to be based on contacts with beings from other worlds who came to the earth on an evangelical mission. The myths of the past are thought to be ancestral memories of visits and mental contacts between alien beings and prehistoric human congregations.

Emanuel Swedenborg was able to travel inward and discover the true meaning of heaven and hell. He heard *and* saw the Other Side. His own personal practice of meditation just happened to be the same method used by the Hindu Yoga and Tibetan Buddhists in their long quests for enlightment. These far eastern religious practices required the individual to concentrate with such power that the outside world would disappear. Swedenborg discovered his dreams would accomplish the same for him as meditation did for Yogas and Buddhists.

The Buddhist is taught how to immerse his attention in a subject just before going asleep. This results in the desired dream state being entered. According to the *Tibetan Book of the Dead*, this kind of concentrated meditation allows one to understand and react favorably to the hereafter when he dies. Swedenborg found that by focusing on the single idea he could develop the hypnogogic dream state. This hypnogogic state is the balance between self-awareness and inner processes. It was the state from which Swedenborg was able to walk in heaven and in hell.

Another person who was able to walk in heaven and in hell on the Other Side was the Danish author Martinus Thomsen, who used the pen name of Martinus. Martinus was working as an accountant in Copenhagen in 1921 when a friend gave him a copy of a book which gave instructions on the Buddhist methods of meditation.

While meditating one evening on "God", Martinus became transformed from a physical to a spiritual entity. He suddenly found his "essence" in the center of a flame and he was quickly confronted with a Christ-figure. He was able to see "God's Kingdom".

Once Martinus learned to remove the body's physical shackles with the help of meditation, he found that the Other Side was a permanent part of his expanded consciousness. He emphasized that he was in complete conscious control of himself in his out-of-body travels and he was at all times completely awake. He continued to meditate and he was able to come to the Godly light and God's consciousness in a "cosmic flash."

Martinus described the Other Side as being composed of different spheres. Purgatory to Martinus, was the place one went to immediately after death. Purgatory was not an especially fearful place, but one composed of vivid surroundings built from the individual's own past experiences. It was a place where one's personality could continue to grow and develop.

Upon leaving purgatory, the soul of the person travelled to the first sphere where the perfect existence was provided. This first sphere was a paradise where people lived and did things for one another. Beyond this first sphere were higher spheres that were composed of spiritual processes and others for the development of learning and artistic endeavors.

Finally, according to what Martinus saw, the spirit of the individual experiences rebirth—a reincarnation of the spirit into another body and with the information of the past life being carried forward for later use and development.

According to the Tibetan Buddhists, as well as other practitioners of meditation, the learned discipline of concentration and focusing upon a single idea helps the person develop the mental orientation to properly face the conditions on the Other Side. Meditation involves an alteration in the way we actually perceive the worlds around us. An important characteristic of this state is the complete absence of visual fantasies. In meditation, attention is concentrated upon a certain point to the exclusion of all other, internal and external, stimuli. It takes a Buddhist a lifetime of constant work and practice to learn the skills necessary to control his thinking.

The technology that is presently available makes it possible for us to learn in an hour the skills of a lifetime of meditation. Electronic instruments are now available which can be attached to the skin of the head and that will read the minute electrical firings that take place in the brain. If the subject is allowed to know of these electrical discharges in some manner, such as a bell or tone, then that subject can actually self-control the firings of his own neurons. Humans are able to alter their own brain wave patterns within an hour or less in the same manner as practioners of yoga. This process of knowing the patterns and attempting to alter their sequence is called biofeedback. It is a method for reaching nirvana.

The Tibetan Book of the Great Liberation (also called *Realizing Nirvana through Knowing the Mind* and the common title *The Tibetan Book of the Dead*) is the guidebook for the hereafter. It gives instructions for the dead on how to behave on the Other Side. *The Great Liberation* was written by Padma-Sambhava. In the 1954 edition, Carl Jung, the psychologist, wrote a psychological interpretation for the book. Jung wrote that the "conflict between science and religion is in reality a misunderstanding of both. Scientific materialism has merely introduced a new hypothesis, and that is an intellectual sin." Jung felt that the *Great Liberation* was a useful guidebook for western man, including scientists. Science "has given another name to the supreme principle of reality and has assumed that this created a new thing and destroyed an old thing. Whether you call the principle of existence 'God,' 'matter,' 'energy,' or anything else you like, you have created nothing; you simply changed a symbol."

The Tibetan Book of the Great Liberation/Dead is a roadmap to the future worlds in terms of future living. It tells the Buddhist what to expect, what to do now to prepare for it, and how to act when they enter Bar-do. Bar-do is the state between death and the later rebirth. Bar-do lasts upwards of 49 days symbolically, but may go on indefinitely for thousands of years. In Bar-do the consciousness of the newly dead comes upon visions of good and bad deities who interact with his consciousness. The form of this interaction is shaped by his own past. In the text, which is read to the dying, the newly dead are to experience a "clear light." If the person has been a good and diligent practitioner of the yogic discipline, he may hold onto the stage where he meets the clear light, and he will not have to experience the rebirth.

To save oneself from being reborn, the Tibetan Buddhist was taught to know his inner self through meditation. Padma-Sambhava wrote concerning self-knowing that the best prepared is the one who looks at himself and not at others.

"The greatest conqueror is the Conqueror of Self. The dominion of such a One is not over this world alone, but over worlds and beings, over those who are not yet men, over those who have grown to manhood, and over those who are gods. It is by looking within, in true oriental manner, not by looking without, that the highway to Universality and Omnipotence and Freedoms are discoverable." (Padma-Sambhava, *The Tibetan Book of the Great Liberation*.)

One source of information to both Sigmund Freud and Carl Jung were dreams. Any truth to be found in a person's accounts of the hereafter are thought to be found in the interpretation of dreams. Jung studied dreams and their influences on people and came to the conclusion that dreaming was the source of all unconscious thoughts. Jung felt that the unconscious mind had the closer touch to the Other Side than did the conscious mind. Freud felt that dreams revealed potentional problems in the person's personality. Jung considered the visions of a dreamer as clues to death and the hereafter. Dreaming was a release from the constraints of this physical reality into the mystical realm of the next one. Tibetan Buddhists are instructed on how to structure their dreams for the greatest possible effect. Patricia Garfield also gives about the same information in her popular book, *Creative Dreaming*.

The proof and/or the acceptance of the Other Side will ultimately be revealed to you. You may experience it beforehand, some scholars think, through the process of altering your states of consciousness—clinical death, near death situations, dreaming, drugs, deathbed visions, meditation, etc. The window to view the Other Side is available for those who have the desire to see what awaits them in the next world.

Samuel T. Coleridge, the English poet and critic, wrote: "What if you slept? And what if, in your sleep, you dreamed? And what if, in your dream you went to heaven and there plucked a strange and beautiful flower? And what if, when you awoke, you had the flower in your hand? Ah, what then?"

The easiest way to glimpse the Other Side, according to Nils Jacobson, is through dreaming. In writing about astral projection, Jacobson believes that the separation of body and soul is the key idea behind the immortality of the human spirit. "During sleep and in certain other circumstances the astral body can free itself from the physical body and move freely in the astral plane."

As far back as man's first beginnings here on earth, mankind has been experiencing the Other Side in dreams. In 1796, John MacGowan wrote about his process of meditating which allowed him to make repeated visits to the Other Side. MacGowan wrote about his travels in his book, *Death, a Vision: or the Solemn Departure of Saints and Sinners*, published in 1796.

"As I was meditating on these awful subjects death, gentle slumber seized me with its lulling charms, and soon wafted me into the arms of downy sleep, where I lay the rest of the night inactive in body, Death having imprinted his image upon me."

"I dreamed that in one place I beheld the most beautiful

garden, that ever I had seen he described it as a place with flowers of all kinds, a lake which burneth with fire and brimstone, where the worm dieth not, and where the fire is not quenched.''

"I found myself in the middle of a spacious field decorated with all the variety of nature, in bloom, . . . revised with the fragrency of the full blown flowers. I beheld the glory of the divine Creator. . . .''

MacGowan saw the spirit of a dead woman enter the Kingdom of Heaven. The woman said, '' 'Come Father Come; Thou knowest I am waiting they command.' '—in a few moments after she quietly departed, and her glorified soul joined the fellowship of heaven. Now, swift as thought they carried her to the blissful regions of eternal day; where she was received with joyful acclamations by all the hosts of the heaven of heavens.'' Once MacGowan awoke, he continued to think about his experiences. "Yea, after all, perhaps to be tired of this world, and yet afraid to venture to another.'' Evidence has now been brought to us by the clinically dead and those on their deathbeds that there is something to the idea of the hereafter. Psychiatrists are no longer placing people into the category of schizophrenics and psychotics when they report their experiences in another dimension. More and more people, are now stepping forward to tell about their own travels now that the stigma of insanity is being lifted from their experiences. Dr. Elisabeth Kubler-Ross and Dr. Raymond Moody are both believers. You also may become a believer in the Other Side.

POSTSCRIPT

The Other Side awaits all of us. It even awaits those who have died and been resuscitated. Mr. Victor Solow was one such individual. His experience of dying affected me. I liked Mr. Solow. He died for a second time on Sunday morning, January 9, 1977. He told me last summer that he really did not want to be brought back from the Other Side. He was a beautiful person and I regret that I did not know him better. I think that he waits for us on the Other Side.

NOSTALGIA

23930 Facts About the Presidents   Kane $1.95
42821 Kane Book of Famous First Facts and Records—1976 Edition Kane $1.95

01625 All in Color for a Dime
 Lupoff and Thompson $1.50

01725 All-Time Great Sports Quiz
 Albi, Bowen & Bailey $1.25

29290 Glad You Asked That! Vol. 1
 Gardner $1.50

30212 Great Child Stars Parish $1.75

30210 Great Westerns Stars Parish $1.75

32301 The Heavyweight Champions
 Weston $1.75

88080 Whatever Became of . . .? Vol. III
 Lamparski $1.50

88627 Why Did They Name It?
 Campbell $1.50

37381 Is That Who I Think It Is? Vol. I   Agan $1.25
37380 Is That Who I Think It Is? Vol. II   Agan $1.25
37382 Is That Who I Think It Is? Vol. III   Agan $1.75

Available wherever paperbacks are sold or use this coupon.

ENRICHMENT LIBRARY

00420	**The Adventure of Birth** Bing	$1.50
04619	**Bachelor Fatherhood** McFadden	$1.50
34489	**How to Find a Job** Larson	$1.95
*03102	**The Art of Vegetarian Cookery** Wason	$1.25
22720	**How To Stop Fighting With Your Kids** Dreikurs	$1.50
23901	**The First Babyfood Cookbook** Morris	$1.50
27961	**Chuang Tzu: Genius of the Absurd** Waltham	$1.50
35866	**I Ching** Translated by C. Waltham	$1.50
51663	**Malpractice and You** Barchilon	$1.75
58101	**Nine Months to Go** Klein	$1.25
*66391	**The Pills in Your Life** Halberstam	$1.50
*67510	**Positive Self Analysis Book I** Singer	$1.50

Available wherever paperbacks are sold or use this coupon.

 ace books, (Dept. MM) Box 576, Times Square Station
New York, N.Y. 10036

Please send me titles checked above.

I enclose $. . . . . Add 35c handling fee per copy.

Name . . . .

Address . . . .

City. . . . . State . . . . Zip . . . .

62A

Over 650 pages of fascinating and unusual information with thousands of facts, dates, names and specifics!

THE KANE BOOK OF

FAMOUS FIRST FACTS AND RECORDS

Contained in one volume — all you ever wanted to know about 20,000 subjects, but never knew how to find!

by Joseph Nathan Kane

Available wherever paperbacks are sold or use this coupon.
